MW01062055

WHEN IT SEEMS ALL HOPE IS GONE

Discover How To Regain Your Faith and Restore Your Life

by Richard Roberts

Harrison House
Tulsa, Oklahoma

10 09 08 07 06   10 9 8 7 6 5 4 3 2 1

When It Seems All Hope Is Gone:
Discover How To Regain Your Faith and Restore Your Life
ISBN 1-57794-202-7
Copyright © 2006 by Oral Roberts Evangelistic Association
Tulsa, Oklahoma 74171-0001

Published by Harrison House, Inc.
P.O. Box 35035
Tulsa, Oklahoma 74153

Table of Contents

Introduction

I remember when I was growing up, my parents never had to worry much about locking our doors. We didn't have to. Today is another story. You wouldn't dream of leaving your home without making sure all of the windows were closed and the doors were locked. My, how times have changed. Gone also are the days where you could work for a business your entire life and expect to have a decent retirement. Between mismanagement of funds and corporations going bankrupt, retirement accounts don't have the security they once did.

Since 9-11, the world has entered into a new realm of insecurity. From heightened security at airports to metal detectors becoming commonplace at most public events, we can never go back to the idyllic days of my childhood.

Where does your hope lie when the world around you seems to be falling apart? Because of the world in which we live, many people feel as though they are hurtling like a meteor straight into the middle of hellish situations. As a result, their hope seems gone. But I have good news. You can firmly put your trust in the Lord Jesus Christ. He will never let you down. It's through the power of His shed blood and the Word of God that you can be sustained when your hope is severely tested.

Hell can break loose at a moment's notice to rob you of your hope and trust in God. Sometimes you can feel the hot breath of hell nipping at your heels, and many times you can smell the sweet breath of heaven just beyond your fingertips. When these situations sweep over your life, there are many things that can keep you tangled in the devil's snare.

Intimidation may enclose its deadly grip on you, or Satan may try to attack you with guilt and condemnation.

That's when he holds your past up before you like a mirror and laughingly mocks you with it. You don't have to live with Satan's condemnation. The Bible says, "There is therefore now no condemnation to those who are in Christ Jesus" (Rom. 8:1).

Something else that can hold you back is fear. Fear is one of the two master emotions, the other being faith. Satan is the master of fear. However, 2 Timothy 1:7 declares, "God has not given us a spirit of fear, but of power, and of love, and of a sound mind."

Even though the fires of hell may be crackling all around you, you can break free from the devil's snare. You can shatter his bonds of intimidation and cast aside fear and condemnation. You can march through the flames of adversity with your shoulders back and your head held high.

Isaiah 43:2 proclaims, "...when you walk through the fire, you shall not be burned, nor shall the flame scorch you." The winds may howl, the fires may rage, and the hammers may pound, but God has promised that our hair will not be singed, and there will be no smell of smoke on our clothing. (Dan. 3:27.)

You can make a determined decision that even though hell may be coming at you, you will not bow your knee to it.

I know what it's like to go through rough waters on a daily basis. When I first became president of ORU, I felt as though I would drown in a torrential flood of financial problems, but by placing my trust in the Lord and planting my seeds of faith to Him, I was able to discover His joy.

This book is a chronicle of how, when my hope seemed gone, the joy of the Lord came alive in my life, how Holy Ghost revival fires erupted at Oral Roberts University, and how I became another man through the baptism of joy.

It's also an account of ORU's journey out of financial bondage. The book of Exodus gives us a panoramic sweep of Israel's exodus from the land of Egypt. It paints a picture of the Lord's provision—how He supplied fresh manna every day, even in the middle of the wilderness. The children of Israel had to believe for that manna to rain down from the sky every day.

I know exactly how that feels. During our financial struggle, there were times when I felt as though all hope was lost and that I was plowing a hole through the sky with my prayers. I've stood eyeball to eyeball with the devil, trying to hold off his deathblows against ORU. Yet, time and again, at the zero hour—at the 11:59 hour—fresh manna, fresh provisions, came flooding down from heaven.

I am mad at the devil because of the attacks he has unleashed against God's people. Every day we're flooded with letters and phone calls from people who are hurting. Their lives are being devastated. Satan is trying to kill their children and them. He has put cancer, heart disease, and other dreaded diseases on their bodies. He has stolen their finances, peace of mind, and joy. I'm tired of seeing this kind of onslaught against the body of Christ. We're God's people, and He did not create us to live in a constant state of disaster.

Yes, trials do come our way. Accidents do happen. But when hell comes at us from every direction, I believe it's a direct strategic plot from Satan himself. Jesus said in Matthew 11:12 that the kingdom of heaven suffers violence from Satan's forces, and we believers have to be violent in our faith to take back the things that Satan has stolen from us.

I believe that as you read this book you are going to be infused with hope and giant-killing faith. A holy indignation is going to be stirred up in you against the devil, and you're going to use your faith to blow up all of his plots and plans.

I've poured out my heart to you through this book, sharing the staggering details of how we almost lost Oral Roberts University, how God began to break us free from Satan's deadly grip, and how we became new people in Christ through a fresh baptism of the joy of the Lord. God's mighty joy and holy laughter have revolutionized my life—and they can do the same for you.

Do you need a new, hilariously happy Holy Ghost revolution in your life? Do you need to learn how to laugh when there's absolutely no reason to laugh? Do you want to be filled with spontaneous, uncontrollable joy, even when the thunder is rolling and the lightning is ripping across the sky of your life? If you do, then don't wait another moment to plunge into this book, because I believe it will revolutionize your life in Christ.

Chapter 1

Stopping the Devil in His Tracks

In 2 Chronicles 20, the armies of the kings of Ammon, Moab, and Mount Seir declared war on King Jehoshaphat and were threatening to destroy every living thing in Israel. When word reached Jehoshaphat that a great multitude was coming against him from beyond the Dead Sea, he was terrified and badly shaken. He was a normal human being like you and me. When adversity came his way, he got scared. Fear gripped him in the pit of his stomach. What set Jehoshaphat apart from most people was that before he would throw his hope away, verse 3 says that he "set" himself to seek the Lord. He made up his mind to seek God's help.

Notice that he didn't first call on his counselors and wise men or ask his top military aides to devise a strategy. Before he consulted anyone, he cried out to God. Let me ask you this question. In the midst of whatever you're going through right now, while Satan is roaring his threats at you, are you seeking the Lord?

Jehoshaphat "set" himself. Eagles have a way of setting their wings against the storm so that when the winds howl and beat against their feathers, they can soar above the storm. Isaiah 40:31 declares that if we seek the Lord and wait upon Him, we, too, shall renew our strength and mount up with wings like eagles.

Jehoshaphat then called on the whole nation to join him in seeking God. Second Chronicles 20:4 declares, "So Judah gathered together to ask help from the Lord...." Jehoshaphat and the Israelites were no

1

WHEN IT SEEMS ALL HOPE IS GONE

match for the great hoards that were marching toward them. It was the David versus Goliath story all over again. In the natural there was no way they could survive the attack. The children of Israel were familiar with those kinds of odds, and they trusted God. Jehoshaphat cried out in verse 6, "O Lord God of our fathers, are You not God in heaven?"

In other words, he was saying, "God, You have not fallen off the throne. Even though our enemies have set themselves in array against us, we know that You are still God." Then the king said, "Are You not God in heaven, and do You not rule over all the kingdoms of the nations?" He was saying, "God, aren't You the One who is still in control?" Next he added, "and in Your hand is there not power and might, so that no one is able to withstand You?"

So many times we feel as if the devil's forces outnumber God's forces. Let me remind you that when Satan fell, he took only one-third of the angels with him. That means there are still two-thirds of the angels who are on assignment on our behalf.

In verse 7 Jehoshaphat continued, "Are You not our God, who drove out the inhabitants of this land before Your people Israel, and gave it to the descendants [seed] of Abraham Your friend forever?" In other words, "Didn't You drive out the inhabitants so the children of Israel might have their inheritance, the kingdom of God?"

Oh, I love what Jehoshaphat said next. He declared, "If calamity comes upon us, whether the sword of judgment, or plague or famine, we will stand in your presence before this temple that bears your Name and will cry out to you in our distress, and you will hear us and save us" (v. 9 NIV). He was saying, "God, if we catch hell from our enemies, we're going to run to You, and You will deliver us."

If I could drive home only one thought to you, it would be this: God loves it when His children run to Him when hard times come their way.

When it looks as if your life is falling apart at the seams, remember to run toward God.

What a hardcore declaration of faith Jehoshaphat made that day. He said, "God, when our hope seems gone, we're going to run to You, and You're going to save us." No ifs, ands, buts, or maybe sos. He wasn't saying, "God, I *hope* You're going to deliver us," or, "I *pray* You're going to deliver us," but, "You *will* deliver us."

He went on to plead his case before the Lord. In verses 10 and 11 Jehoshaphat said, "And now, here are the people of Ammon, Moab, and Mount Seir—whom You would not let Israel invade when they came out of the land of Egypt, but they turned from them and did not destroy them—here they are, rewarding us by coming to throw us out of Your possession which You have given us to inherit." In other words, the king was saying, "Look God, You wouldn't let us invade these nations or destroy their armies. But now they come to throw us out of the land that You have given us."

Is that the way you feel sometimes? Do you feel as if you've been obedient to what the Lord has told you to do, but now the devil is doing his best to tear it away from you? Then you need to keep on reading and see what Jehoshaphat did to bring a great deliverance into his life.

In verse 12 he proclaimed, "O our God, will You not judge them?" Think about someone who may be speaking evil about you or perhaps even striking out to hurt you. Then declare, "O God, will You not judge them?" You're saying, "God, they're not my problem anymore. You'll take care of them. You'll judge them." You and I don't need to get into judgment. Sometimes we may *feel* like pounding our fist into a wall or hitting someone. I always tell my wife, Lindsay, "You have to *cast* the devil out of people. You can't *beat* the devil out of them."

The Power of Praise

Jehoshaphat cried out to the Lord, "For we have no power against this great multitude that is coming against us" (v. 12). Isn't that the way you feel when you experience hardship? You feel as if you have no might and no strength when he sends his satanic onslaught against your life.

Listen to what Jehoshaphat said next: "nor do we know what to do, but our eyes are upon You" (v. 12). There have been many times in my life when I didn't have the slightest idea of what to do. The Bible says that when we don't know what to pray for or how to pray as we should, that's when we should pray in tongues. (Rom. 8:26.)

Jehoshaphat was saying, "God, we don't have any well-trained military forces to take on this vast enemy. We don't have any superior firepower. We don't have any Patriot missiles or modern-day weapons or artillery. God, unless You tell us what to do, we're sunk."

In verse 14 the Bible says that the Spirit of the Lord came upon one of the men who had gathered around Jehoshaphat to pray. It's important for you to realize that the Bible gives us this man's credentials. It says, "Then the Spirit of the Lord came upon Jahaziel the son of Zechariah, the son of Benaiah, the son of Jeiel, the son of Mattaniah, a Levite of the sons of Asaph, in the midst of the assembly."

Why do you suppose this Scripture gives us so much information about this particular man? God wants us to know something about the people who give us a word from the Lord. If someone you've never met before walks up to you and gives you a word about your life that doesn't confirm something God has already spoken to your heart, put it on the back burner. If it's truly from God, it *will* come to pass as you obey God.

The Scripture tells us that this man, Jahaziel, was not only a Levite, a member of the priestly tribe, but he was also a descendant of Asaph, who was King David's own praise and worship leader. Jahaziel was a priest unto the Lord, a minister of God; and when he spoke a word by the Spirit, the people had every reason to believe that it was true.

Jahaziel said, "Listen, King Jehoshaphat and all who live in Judah and Jerusalem! This is what the Lord says to you: 'Do not be afraid or discouraged because of this vast army. For the battle is not yours, but God's. Tomorrow march down against them. They will be climbing up by the Pass of Ziz, and you will find them at the end of the gorge in the Desert of Jeruel. You will not have to fight this battle. Take up your positions; stand firm and see the deliverance the Lord will give you, O Judah and Jerusalem. Do not be afraid; do not be discouraged. Go out to face them tomorrow, and the Lord will be with you'" (vv. 15-17 NIV).

What a powerful word from God. Can you imagine how you would feel if you thought you were about to be wiped out by your enemies and the Lord said something like that to you? One of the amazing things about this Scripture is the fact that the prophet told them the exact location of the enemy forces. I believe God will reveal Satan's strategies to us in advance, too.

When Jehoshaphat heard that word, he was so grateful and in awe of God's goodness and mercy that he bowed his head with his face to the ground, and all the people of Judah and Jerusalem fell down in worship before the Lord. Then the Bible says that some of the Levites stood up and began to praise the Lord "…with a very loud voice" (v. 19 NIV). They had a Holy Ghost praise service right there on the spot.

Early the next morning, Jehoshaphat addressed the people, saying, "Believe in the Lord your God, so shall ye be established; believe his prophets, so shall ye prosper" (v. 20).

It's important for you to get hold of this spiritual principle for your deliverance. When you receive a word from the Lord through one of His prophets, or even a word that God may speak in your own spirit, you've got to latch on to that word by faith. You've got to grab hold of it and believe, because your faith is what activates that word in your life. If you're in a church service or you're attending a healing crusade and a minister of the Gospel speaks a prophetic word, you can either receive that word as a personal word for your life, or you can let it float by you. The choice is yours.

Jehoshaphat is saying, "If you believe the word God's prophet speaks to you, if you accept it by faith and take hold of it in your life, you will prosper." On the other hand, if you let that word pass you by, it's not going to bring any success into your life.

What Jehoshaphat did next was highly unconventional. The Bible says that he consulted with the people before he sent them into battle. That's an unusual thing for a king to do. I thank God for leaders who stay in touch with those they lead.

After he had consulted with the people, the king appointed praise and worship leaders to lead the army into battle. The Bible says, "Jehoshaphat appointed men to sing to the Lord and to praise him for the splendor of his holiness" (v. 21 NIV). *The Amplified Bible* says that the singers went out in their priestly garments before the army, declaring, "Give thanks to the Lord, for His mercy and lovingkindness endure for ever!"

This is the most unconventional warfare I've ever heard of. Here is the fierce Israeli army marching out to meet the armies of Moab, Ammon, and Mount Seir. Can you imagine those powerful Israeli soldiers flashing their bayonets and swords and knives while a praise and worship team marched out in front of them? Now that's unusual.

I wonder what would have happened if the American commander of the allied forces during the recent war in Iraq had sent praise and worship singers to lead the infantry as they marched toward Baghdad. What if the power and might of the Lord had come upon those soldiers and right in front of their tanks and guns, their artillery and mortars, they had sent up praises to God? Just think of what the news media would have done with that story.

Psalm 22:3 says that God inhabits the praises of His people. I believe we've taken that Scripture far too lightly in the past. We simply haven't grasped how earthshaking it really is to praise the Lord. Think about it for a moment. God Almighty, the Creator of heaven and earth, lives in, dwells in, and manifests His presence through our praises. That means all the supernatural forces of our God skyrocket into action when we praise Him. This Scripture is not talking about the sweet presence of the Lord settling over the congregation like a cloud. It's talking about our all-powerful Savior, the Lord of hosts, wiping out our enemies with one blast from His nostrils.

God Will Fight for You

When the sound of Israel's praises reached the ears of God Almighty, He set ambushes against the armies of Ammon, Moab, and Mount Seir, "and they were smitten" (2 Chron. 20:22 KJV). What does *smitten* mean? It means "to kill or severely injur."[1] Israel's enemies fell into such frenzy that they began to turn on each other and slaughter one another. When the men of Judah reached the battlefield, the Bible says, "They saw only dead bodies lying on the ground; no one had escaped" (v. 24 NIV).

I tell you, when God turns on the devil's pack, not one of them escapes. Not only that, but Israel didn't have to lift a finger to fight. They simply had to obey God and march out to the battlefield. They just had to show up and praise the Lord no matter how bleak things looked.

There were such vast heaps of spoils that it took the soldiers three days to gather up all the abundance of valuables and precious jewelry. Thank God, Jehoshaphat didn't forget about the Lord as soon as He

---

[1] *Merriam-Webster's Online Dictionary*, s.v. "smite."

7

gave them the victory. The Bible says that after the men had finished gathering up the spoils, they assembled in the Valley of Beracah and began to shout loud praises unto God. Then Jehoshaphat led his army back to Jerusalem in a joyful Jericho victory march. (vv. 25-27.)

The fear of the Lord came upon all the surrounding nations when they heard how God had fought against the enemies of Israel and defeated them. "And the kingdom of Jehoshaphat was at peace, for his God had given him rest on every side" (v. 30 NIV). *Today's English Version* says, "Jehoshaphat ruled in peace, and God gave him security on every side."

Isn't that what you want in your life, security on every side? I'm talking about the kind of security that only God can give. When hellish situations surround you from every side, you don't have to let them rob you of your hope. Begin to praise the Lord and expect God's angels to give you security round about.

Chapter 2

Staying Out of Satan's Traps

The best example in the Bible of someone who slipped into a trap of Satan is Samson, a man of unmatched strength. The birth of Samson was supernatural. His mother had been barren all of her married life until one day she was visited by an angel. He revealed to her that she was going to have a son, and he also gave her divine instructions concerning the child. (Judg. 13.)

The angel commanded her not to drink wine or strong drink while she was carrying the baby or to eat anything that was contrary to the Jewish dietary laws. He also instructed her not to cut her son's hair for he was to be a Nazarite from his birth, or one separated unto God. He further explained that the child was destined to deliver Israel from the Philistines.

At that particular time, because of their disobedience to the Lord, the people of God were being dominated by ungodly and cruel men. Nobody likes to be roughed up by a bully or shoved around by his enemies. No doubt the Israelites had been crying out to God for a deliverer, and He answered their cry by sending Samson.

Even as a young man, when the Spirit of the Lord came upon Samson, he could perform great feats of strength. Unfortunately, he also had a terrible weakness, and Satan used his weakness to put a hook into his nose and make him the laughingstock of the entire Philistine nation.

In Judges 14, you'll notice that Samson was troubled by lust for heathen women. One day he strolled into the Philistine camp where he spotted a beautiful young woman. He was so strongly attracted to her that

9

he told his father and mother, "Get her for me as a wife" (v. 2). Samson's father was shocked by his request. He was a devout Jewish man, and he wanted his son to marry a young Jewish woman. Besides, he knew that the hand of the Lord was upon Samson, and if he married someone of his own faith, it would be much easier for him to pursue his calling.

Strangely enough, the Bible says in verse 4 that the Lord was behind Samson's request to marry this Philistine girl because He was setting a trap to stir up a fight between Samson and the Philistines, who at that time ruled Israel. Isn't it amazing how God can use even our weaknesses to get us into a position to do what He's called us to do?

While Samson and his parents were on their way to make arrangements for Samson's marriage, the Bible says that a young lion came against him from the forest. Like a bolt of lightning, the Spirit of the Lord came upon Samson, and he tore the lion to pieces with his bare hands. He and his parents then continued on their way to meet his young bride's family.

As soon as Samson talked with the girl, his heart leaped with joy. Surely she was the one for him. The preparations were made for the marriage, and Samson and his parents returned home. Later, when they were on their way back for the wedding, Samson decided to stop and look at the carcass of the lion. He was startled to discover that a swarm of bees had built a hive in its decaying body. He scooped up some of the honey and took it to his parents, but he didn't tell anyone where it came from.

At the wedding feast, it was customary for several of the young men to accompany the groom. The Philistines gave Samson a bachelor's party; and for the next seven days, he and thirty young men were constant companions. In order to amuse himself, Samson decided to tell them a riddle. He wagered each of his young Philistine companions a piece of fine linen and a change of fine clothing that none of them could answer his riddle by the end of the wedding feast. He declared, "Out of the eater came forth meat, and out of the strong came forth sweetness" (v. 14 KJV).

Of course, he was referring to the honey that came forth from the carcass of the lion. Three days later they were still trying to solve the riddle. The young Philistines were so upset by Samson's challenge that they threatened his new wife, saying, "Entice your husband, that he may explain the riddle to us, or else we will burn you and your father's house with fire" (v. 15).

Naturally, she was terrified by their threats. She burst into tears before Samson and cried, "'You only hate me! You do not love me! You have posed a riddle to the sons of my people, but you have not explained it to me.' And he said to her, 'Look, I have not explained it to my father or my mother; so should I explain it to you?'" (v. 16).

I want to point out two more weaknesses which often plagued Samson's life. First, he confided in people in whom he never should have confided. And second, he let people badger him until they wore down his resolve and pressured him into doing things he really did not want to do.

Beware of anyone who tries to probe into your private thoughts and secrets. They may be well-meaning friends who only want to help you, but they also may have their own agenda. They may be weaving their own cunning plot to harm you. That's why the Bible tells us to be "...wise as serpents and harmless as doves" (Matt. 10:16). A wise man knows when to keep his mouth shut.

Samson's wife cried and pitched a fit until he finally revealed to her the meaning of the riddle. She immediately told his Philistine companions, and they reported the answer back to him. Samson was furious when he discovered that his wife had betrayed him. The Bible says that the Spirit of the Lord came upon him, and he killed thirty Philistines from another town, stripped them of their fine clothing, and gave their clothes to the men who had answered his riddle. Then he left his wife at her father's house and went back home in a huff.

Later, after he had cooled off, Samson decided to take a present to his wife to see if he could smooth things over. (Judg. 15.) Actually, he wanted to spend the night with her, but her father informed him that he had already given her to Samson's best man. Then he offered to give Samson one of his other daughters to be his wife, but Samson wouldn't hear of it.

He flew into such a violent rage that he went out and trapped three hundred foxes, tied their tails together in pairs, and stuck torches into the knots. Then he lit the torches and drove the foxes through the Philistines' cornfields. Not only did the fire ravage the corn crops, but it also torched the vineyards and olive trees.

When the Philistines found out that Samson had attacked them to avenge himself for his father-in-law's actions, they got the girl and her father and burned them to death. That only outraged Samson further, and he attacked and killed more Philistines, then fled and hid in a cave. (v. 6.)

God didn't want those terrible things to happen to the father-in-law and his daughter, but remember, the Bible says the hand of the Lord was moving behind the scenes—to stir up a war between Samson and the Philistines. God wanted to use Samson to set His people free. That tells me that He can use unexpected circumstances to cause His will to come to pass in your life. The key is for you to keep your heart pure and your spirit sensitive to Him. He can use even the most unusual circumstances to give you an outstanding victory.

Don't Let the Devil Wear You Down

While Samson was in his hideout, the Philistines raided a town in Judah. When the men of Judah asked them what had provoked the attack, the Philistines replied, "We've come to capture Samson and do to him what he did to us." Three thousand men from Judah tracked down Samson and demanded to know, "What have you done to us? Are you trying to destroy us? Don't you realize that the Philistines are our rulers?"

Finally, Samson agreed to let his countrymen take him captive, but he made them promise they wouldn't kill him. They bound Israel's champion with heavy new ropes and delivered him to the Philistines. At that instant God's power surged through Samson's body, and he snapped those ropes in two like they were made of thread.

I can imagine the Philistines recoiling with fear when they realized that Samson had broken free. I can hear them gasping in horror as they watched him walk out into their midst, swinging the jawbone of a donkey as his only weapon, the fire of God flashing in his eyes. In a matter of moments, a thousand Philistines lay dead at Samson's feet. It was a terrible bloodbath.

Afterwards, Samson became extremely thirsty, and he cried out to the Lord for a drink of water. God opened a hollow place in the jawbone, causing a stream of water to gush forth, and Samson's spirit was revived as he drank.

I want you to picture this scene. Here was Samson, a man who had witnessed the awesome, miracle-working power of God in action, a man who was greatly gifted of the Lord. He was walking knee-deep in miracles. How could such a man sink to the depths to which he sank? More importantly, how can you and I resist Satan's traps so we don't follow in Samson's footsteps? Or, if you've already slipped and stumbled in some area of your life, how can you find your way back to the right path?

Remember, Satan doesn't wear us down in a single day or drag us into a pit overnight. We don't wake up one morning and suddenly discover that our lives are shattered, and we're catching hell because of our mistakes and sins.

Satan began to chisel away at Samson's character a little bit at a time. Perhaps he built up his ego by telling him what a great man he was, what a powerful, manly warrior. Maybe he appealed to Samson's pride.

WHEN IT SEEMS ALL HOPE IS GONE

Of course, he constantly eroded his judgment concerning women. As Satan played the tune, Samson began to dance.

The devil lured him into the bed of a prostitute in the city of Gaza. (Judg. 16.) When the Philistines learned that Samson was there, they locked the gates of the city. Once again the Spirit of the Lord came upon him, and he ripped the massive gates off their hinges and carried them to the top of the hill overlooking Mount Hebron.

Later, Samson met a Philistine woman named Delilah. She must have been a stunning beauty, full of feminine charms, because Satan used her to cast a spell on the deliverer of Israel. Samson instantly fell in love with her, and his love cost him his life. As soon as the five Philistine kings discovered that Delilah was Samson's new lover, they made a deal with her. They told her, "Trick him into telling you the secret of his strength so we will know how to overpower and bind him, and each of us will give you eleven hundred pieces of silver."

Delilah began to quiz him. "Samson, what makes you so strong?" she pleaded, perhaps squeezing his muscles and playing up to his manly pride. Samson began to tease and mock her by giving her false answers. He told her, "If you tie me up with seven leather bowstrings, I'll be as weak as any other man."

While he slept she tied him up with seven leather bowstrings, and then she cried out, "Samson, the Philistines are coming." When he jumped up, he snapped those leather bowstrings as if they were mere strands of yarn. Delilah was furious. "Samson, you've mocked me and told me lies." She screamed at him. "You've got to tell me your secret, or *else.*"

He told her, "If you fasten me with new ropes, I'll be as weak as a kitten." Again as he slept, Delilah eagerly wrapped new ropes around his arms and legs, and then she shouted, "The Philistines are coming." Samson awoke and flexed his muscles, and those ropes scattered in every direction. She might as well have bound him with a piece of ribbon.

Delilah really flared at him that time, yelling, "Samson, you've mocked me again. You've got to stop lying to me. I want to know the truth about your strength."

Then he told her, "If you weave the locks of my hair with a loom, I'll be as weak as any other man." That night, while he was asleep, Delilah braided the seven locks of his hair and wove them upon her loom. Then she called to him, "Samson, the Philistines are upon you." But he jerked his hair out of her loom in one split second.

At last Delilah began to cajole him mercilessly, "Samson, how can you say you love me, when you won't confide in me? This is the third time you've made a fool of me. Why won't you tell me the secret of your great strength?"

Samson forgot what his wife had said: "If you really love me, you'll tell me the answer to your riddle." How short our memory is when Satan is tantalizing our flesh. Delilah nagged him and prodded him day after day until the Bible says, "...he was tired to death" (Judg. 16:16 NIV). She had finally worn him down. Satan loves to wear us down.

The Bible says that Samson finally spilled his guts to her. He said, "I've been dedicated to God as a Nazarite from my birth, and my hair has never been cut. If my hair were cut, I would lose all of my strength." When Delilah realized that Samson had finally told her the truth, she sent for the Philistines. They rushed over and brought the money with them.

That night Delilah lulled Samson to sleep with his head on her lap and called in a Philistine barber to shave off the seven braids of Samson's hair. When the first rays of sunlight streaked through the curtains the next morning, Delilah whispered, "Wake up, Samson. The Philistines are here to capture you." Samson roused himself and thought, *I'll shake myself as I've done so many times before.* He had a way of shaking himself when the Spirit of God came upon him. But the Bible says he didn't know that the Spirit of the Lord had departed from him.

15

When Samson flexed his muscles that day, there was no strength in them. His arms fell limp at his sides. Suddenly the champion of God stood helpless before his enemies.

Resisting the Devil's Temptations

The irony of Samson's story is that he could have won easily against Delilah. All he had to do was walk in the Spirit instead of walking in the flesh. Galatians 5:16 says, "Walk in the Spirit, and you shall not fulfill the lust of the flesh."

This should not have been a difficult battle for a man who could crush a thousand Philistines with the jawbone of a donkey or tear the gates of a great city off their hinges and drag them up a hillside. The battle isn't hard for you and me if we'll use our spiritual weapons, if we'll draw upon the unfailing resources of the Holy Spirit.

How can we resist the lures of the devil? Romans 8:1-14 tells us we must learn to walk in the Spirit and refuse to pursue the things of the flesh. We must sow our seeds to the Spirit instead of sowing seeds to the flesh. In other words, we've got to fill our lives with the things of God—with prayer, with the Word, and with godly fellowship—instead of the things of this world.

It's a spiritual law: What you feed on is what will grow in your life. Galatians 6:8 puts it this way: "He who sows to his flesh will of the flesh reap corruption, but he who sows to the Spirit will of the Spirit reap everlasting life." If you feed on the things of the Spirit, the urges of your flesh will grow weaker and weaker. On the other hand, if you feed on the things of the flesh, they will get a deadly grip on you. You can't afford to play around with sin.

Run From Your Weaknesses

Delilah represents anything or anybody who gets their hooks into us and causes us to let them have mastery over us. I tell you, don't *walk* away from your Delilah. *Run* from her. Whatever Delilah you're facing, flee from it. Run from it in your spirit. Fall upon the mercy of the Lord. Tell God, "I can't handle this by myself, but I know Your Spirit can help me cast it out of my life."

The Philistines pounced upon the mighty deliverer of Israel, shackled him, and gouged out his eyes. They led him away to the city of Gaza, where they threw him into prison. There Samson labored day after day in darkness, hitched up like a beast of burden to a grindstone and forced to grind in a mill. Can you see God's champion, a blind, defeated, and whipped prisoner?

No matter what traps we may stumble into, God is still a good God. The Bible teaches us that He will come to us again. Judges 16:22 says that Samson's hair began to grow. No doubt as he trudged his wearisome path, around and around, grinding in the prison house, one day he must have felt something tickling his neck. When he reached up, he discovered that little wisps of hair were beginning to grow. When Samson felt hair on his neck, he knew God's power was coming back into his life.

One day the Philistines decided to hold a great feast for their god, Dagon, to celebrate their victory over Israel's fallen champion. Someone chimed in, "Let Samson make sport for us." And all the lords and ladies gathered in the temple of Dagon for a great party. They were laughing and drinking and having the time of their lives when a soldier brought Samson from the prison to entertain them.

They made a fatal mistake that day. They made Samson stand between the pillars that supported the temple. He asked the boy who was leading him to put his hands on the pillars. He told him, "I want to lean on them."

The temple was jammed to the rafters as the Philistines shouted praises to their god. Amid the cheers and celebration, they began to jeer at Samson and mock the God of Abraham, Isaac, and Jacob. As Samson leaned upon the pillars, he bowed his head and cried out, "O Sovereign Lord, remember me. O God, please strengthen me just once more, and let me with one blow get revenge on the Philistines for my two eyes" (v. 28). He was saying, "Lord, just let me feel Your power one more time."

Samson prayed, "Let me die with the Philistines!" (v. 29). And like a great burst of wind, the Spirit of God blew through Samson's body, and his arms became like bands of steel. He began to flex his muscles as he leaned into the pillars with all of his might, and the building trembled. Then the Spirit of God touched that cold stone, and the pillars began to pop and crack. Great pieces of plaster crashed to the ground as the stones dislodged and the temple shook and shuddered.

When Samson yanked those pillars out of their sockets, the walls cracked and heaved, and down they came. The temple of Dagon collapsed upon the hissing, jeering Philistines and buried every last one of them beneath the rubble. The great pillars of the temple fell upon Samson, too, but he killed more Philistines in his death than he had killed during his entire lifetime. (v. 29.)

If you're going through a fiery trial, that doesn't mean it's because you've done something wrong or have fallen into sin like Samson did. If what you are experiencing is because of your own faults and shortcomings, God can still visit you with His miracle-working power. He can sweep over your life with the mighty, rushing wind of His Spirit. All you have to do is call upon His name. Ask Him to forgive you, and turn from the things that have bound you in the past. God is a God of a second chance. As long as you keep coming back to Him when you fall, He will always be there to scoop you up in His arms.

Chapter 3

Turning Threats Into Miracles

In 1 Kings 19:4, the prophet Elijah was having a really down time. So much so that he prayed that he would die. He was running for his life from a wild woman named Jezebel, the wickedest queen ever known to Israel, and her death threats had sent him into a tailspin.

If you remember the background of this story found in 1 Kings 17, Elijah had told Jezebel's husband, King Ahab, "As the Lord God of Israel lives, before whom I stand, there shall not be dew nor rain these years, except at my word" (v. 1). As soon as he said those words, the Lord told him to flee for his life. First, he camped beside a brook called Cherith, where he drank from the waters of the brook, and the ravens dropped meat down from the sky for him to eat. When the brook dried up and the ravens stopped flying over, the Lord sent him to a city called Zarephath where God had commanded a widow to sustain him.

When Elijah arrived at the widow's house, she was cooking her last meal. She told him, "I'm going to fry a couple of pancakes for my boy and me, and then we're going to eat them and die." But Elijah replied, "Give me a portion first."

Can you imagine what the *Zarephath Times* would have done with that story? The newspaper headlines might have read: "Prophet Asks for Widow's Last Bit of Food."

Then Elijah gave her the clincher. He said, "Do not fear; go and do as you have said, but make me a small cake from it first, and bring it to me; and afterward make some for yourself and your son. For thus says the Lord God of Israel: 'The bin of flour shall not be used up, nor shall the jar of oil run dry, until the day the Lord sends rain on the earth.'" (vv. 13,14). She obeyed Elijah, and the Bible says that they "did eat many days" (v. 15 KJV)—as long as it was needed—from that near-empty meal barrel and cruse of oil.

Obediently Following God

While Elijah was hiding from King Ahab, the king ordered all of his spies and his secret service agents to comb the countryside to look for the prophet of God. (1 Kings 18.) Ahab blamed Elijah for the terrible drought in Israel. It had really been caused by Ahab and Jezebel when they refused to obey the Lord and led the people to worship Baal. (1 Kings 16:20-34.)

When God finally sent Elijah back to town, he told Ahab to round up the four hundred and fifty prophets of Baal and the four hundred other satanic prophets who ate at Jezebel's table so he could meet them face to face. All the people and the prophets gathered at Mount Carmel, and Elijah proclaimed, "How long are you going to be so wishy-washy about what you believe? How long are you going to pretend that you believe in the one true God while you cling to your superstitions? If God is God, then follow Him, but if Baal is God, then follow him." The Bible says, "The people answered him not a word" (1 Kings 18:21).

Elijah took two bulls, one for the prophets of Baal and one for himself to sacrifice to the Lord. He told them, "Cut your bull into pieces and lay it on the wood, but don't put any fire under it; and I'll do the same with mine. You call on the name of your gods, and I'll call upon the name of the Lord. The God who answers by fire, let him be God."

The prophets of Baal carefully laid their bull upon the altar, and then they began to cry out to their god all morning. Around noon Elijah began to mock them, saying, "Perhaps your god is talking to somebody, or he is on a journey. Or maybe he's asleep." That only made the prophets flail about even more. They jumped and shouted and cut themselves with knives and daggers until the blood gushed out, trying to convince Baal to send down fire. They began to prophesy, but nothing happened. The Bible says that "...there was no reply, no voice, no answer" (v. 29 TLB).

A Demonstration of God's Power

Meanwhile, about sunset, Elijah dug a trench around the altar and got the wood ready. He cut his bull into pieces and laid it on the altar. Then he ordered barrels to be filled with water and poured water over the bull until the water sloshed all the way down the altar and filled the trench.

Elijah didn't cut himself or dance around the altar. He didn't jump, shout, scream, or yell to see if he could get the Lord to answer him. Instead, he called upon the name of his God by saying, "Hear me, O Lord...that this people may know that You are the Lord God" (v. 37). And the fire of the Lord fell.

First, it consumed the bull upon the altar. Then the wood burst into flames, and the flames licked up all the water in the trench. When the people saw it, they immediately fell on their faces and cried out, "The Lord, He is God! The Lord, He is God!" (v. 39.) Next Elijah told the people to seize the prophets of Baal and execute them, just as God had commanded them to do.

Elijah told Ahab, "Go, eat and drink, for I hear the sound of an abundance of rain. I hear thunder and the thunder says that it's going to be a gully washer. It's going to come down in torrents and shake loose the drought. It's going to rain upon the land."

Elijah climbed to the top of Mount Carmel, to the very peak of the mountain, got down on the ground, put his head between his knees, and began to cry out to God for rain. He sent his servant to look out across the Mediterranean Sea for a sign of a cloud. When the servant came back, he said, "There is nothing," but Elijah sent him six more times to look for rain. (v. 43.) The seventh time, the servant exclaimed, "I see a little cloud the size of a man's hand coming out of the sea." That cloud meant everything to Elijah.

He said, "Go tell Ahab to get his chariot ready, so the rain won't stop him." When Ahab heard that word, he jumped in his chariot, pulled by two of the fastest Arabian horses in Israel, and drove with all of his fury to Jezreel. The Bible says that Elijah girded up his loins and raced like the wind across the Plain of Esdraelon. (v. 46.) As the rain pelted down, Elijah ran with all of his might, and he beat Ahab to the gates of the city.

Catching Hell From an Evil Woman

When King Ahab told his wife, Jezebel, what Elijah had done—how he had killed all of her false prophets—she got so mad that she sent a message to Elijah: "So let the gods do to me, and more also, if I do not make your life as the life of one of them by tomorrow about this time" (1 Kings 19:2). She put out a death contract on him.

Elijah caught hell from Jezebel because he had been obedient to the Lord. When you're obedient to the Lord by praising Him, leading people to Jesus, praying for the sick and for people to climb out of wheelchairs and for blind eyes to open, Satan is going to go ballistic. He's not going to be happy about what you are doing. When you're doing the Lord's work, he'll come after you. He came after Elijah through a woman named Jezebel.

When Elijah heard Jezebel's message, fear gripped him, and he fled into the wilderness to a place called Beersheba, which is a little spot way out in the desert, and it's very hot, dusty, and desolate. The Bible says that Elijah traveled a day's journey into the wilderness, sat down under a juniper tree, and began to cry out to the Lord. He said, "God, why don't You just let me die?" Most of us have probably felt that way at some time in our lives. Even Elijah wasn't exempt from that type of feeling.

As he slept, an angel came and touched him and said, "Arise and eat" (v 5). Elijah roused himself, looked around, and saw some cakes baking on hot coals and a jar of water. Didn't the Lord say in Psalm 23:5 that He would prepare a table before you in the presence of your enemies? Elijah got up and ate and drank and lay down again. After he had rested, the angel of the Lord touched him a second time and said, "Arise and eat, because the journey is too great for you" (v. 7).

Elijah wasn't aware that he was about to embark on a great journey for the Lord. All he knew was that he was lying under a juniper tree in the wilderness and he felt like dying. He was obedient to God, but it only produced a death contract on his life. He felt like quitting. He wanted to chuck the whole deal and escape to the farthest place on the face of the earth.

The Bible says, "He arose, and ate and drank; and he went in the strength of that food forty days and forty nights as far as Horeb, the mountain of God" (v. 8). Elijah spent the night on Mount Horeb, hiding in a cave, wrapped in his mantle, and searching for God. When your situation seems hopeless, that's the time you need to seek the Lord.

A Still, Quiet Voice

The word of the Lord came to the prophet Elijah that day and told him, "Go out and stand before Me on the mountain." (v. 11.) Isn't it wonderful that God's word can come to you when the Jezebels in your life rob you of your hope? When Elijah obeyed, the wind started to howl. You talk about a windstorm. The wind roared so hard that the rocks in the mountain began to break into pieces. *Surely this must be the*

Lord talking to me, Elijah thought, but the Bible says that God wasn't in the wind.

The earth beneath his feet began to shake and rumble. Elijah felt the very footing upon which he was standing quake. Perhaps that's the way you feel today—as if the ground is shaking underneath you. Maybe you feel as if your faith and everything in your life is shaking underneath you. Elijah thought the Lord must be in the violent shaking, but the Bible says, "...the Lord was not in the earthquake" (v. 11).

After the earthquake, a fire erupted, and the flames began to shoot upward into the sky. But the Lord wasn't in the fire.

Then Elijah heard a still, small voice whispering to him, saying, "What are you doing here?" The lonely prophet wrapped his face in his mantle and began to rehearse his case before the Lord.

He said, "I have been very zealous for the Lord God of hosts. I have worked my heart out for You, Lord. All the rest of these people have forsaken Your covenant, torn down Your altars, and killed Your prophets, and I'm the only one left. Now Jezebel is trying to kill me too." (v. 14.)

God wasn't moved by Elijah's sad story. He asked him, "Why are you having a pity party? Why are you feeling so sorry for yourself? Why are you so upset because Jezebel wants to cut your head off?"

You will find Jezebels wherever you go. Somebody will show up and try to stop the move of God in your life. There's always somebody who wants to stop you from prospering, who wants to stop you from experiencing the presence of the Lord in your life. God said to Elijah, "Don't pay any attention to the Jezebels of life. Don't let them get to you. You've got a great work to do for Me. Stop lying in that puddle of tears. Get down off this mountain and do what I've commanded you to do."

God was saying, "Elijah, when the devil tries to steal your hope, don't let him. Don't get sidetracked. Just get on with your work for the Lord, because I have a great plan for your life." Elijah obeyed the voice of the Lord and went on about his business, which included anointing a young man named Elisha, who would someday take Elijah's place and do twice as many miracles in the name of the Lord.

It's easy for us to look at the circumstances that surround us instead of focusing on the Lord. When you take your eyes off the Lord and what He said in His Word, the devil will easily steal your hope. However, when you keep your eyes locked on the One who gives you victory in every area, you will overcome every situation the devil brings your way.

Chapter 4

Jesus' Example for Combating the Devil

When Jesus stepped into the muddy waters of the Jordan River to be baptized by John the Baptist, He did it in obedience to God's Word. In the next instant, the heavens opened and the Holy Ghost appeared like a dove and fluttered down to earth, landing on the Lord. "Suddenly a voice came from heaven, saying, 'This is My beloved Son, in whom I am well pleased'" (Matt. 3:17).

The word of prophecy of old was fulfilled when John dipped Jesus under the water of the Jordan. The Bible says, "Then Jesus, being filled with the Holy Spirit, returned from Jordan and was led by the Spirit into the wilderness" (Luke 4:1).

Two things happened when Jesus obeyed God's Word through His baptism. The Bible says that He was full of the Holy Ghost and that He was led by the Spirit into the wilderness. In Mark's gospel it says that the Holy Spirit drove Him into the wilderness. (Mark 1:12.) That is *not* a picture of God's Spirit gently nudging Jesus along the wilderness highway. *The Living Bible* says that Jesus was "…urged by the Spirit out into the barren wastelands of Judea" (Luke 4:1). There was an urgency about the Spirit's promptings.

I want you to imagine this scene from the Word of God: The Holy Spirit is driving the Lord Jesus Christ into the barren wastelands of Judea. He's pressing Him to complete His mission for the Father. Most people shudder when they think about God's Spirit *sending* them on a mission to a barren wasteland, much less *driving* them toward their destination with great force.

Let's take this one step further. Another translation says that the Spirit of God led Jesus into the desert "...in order to be tempted by the devil" (Matt. 4:1 WEYMOUTH). Not only did the Spirit of God lead Jesus into the wilderness and drive Him into a barren wasteland, but He drove Him there for the express purpose of being tempted by Satan. What on earth was going on here?

When Jesus was full of the Holy Ghost, the tempter came. It's important for you to recognize that when you're full of the Holy Spirit and the anointing of God is upon you, that's when the tempter comes. If you're walking side by side with the devil, you'll never meet him face to face. It's only when you're doing something for God that you meet him head-on.

How did the tempter come against Jesus? He came against His flesh. Jesus was led into a desert wilderness by the Holy Spirit, and for forty days and forty nights Satan badgered and harassed Him. During that time, the Bible says that Jesus fasted.

The only other person in the Bible who fasted for that length of time was the prophet Moses, so this is not a pattern that's being held up as a biblical example for us today. Of course, there may be special times when we feel led to fast a meal here and there, or we may occasionally fast for a day or two at a time. The apostle Paul said he fasted often. (2 Cor. 11:27.) Short, regular fasts are the types of fasts which are held up as the model for New Testament believers.

Jesus fasted for forty days and nights while continually being tempted by the devil. Can you imagine how you would feel if you had fasted for that long? No doubt you would be exhausted and barely able to hold your head up. You would be famished. With that in mind, I want you to picture Jesus at the end of forty days in a desert wilderness, without food, trying to stand up, His body weak and His strength wasted. After

He had struggled to His feet, He glanced around, and there was the tempter, staring Him in the face.

Notice that the devil came against Jesus when He was at His weakest physically. Don't think for a moment that Satan is going to come against you when you're operating at full force. He always comes when there is some kind of weakness he can latch onto. He is always searching for a way to get his tentacles wrapped around you.

Jesus was weak with hunger when Satan came at Him, saying, "If You really are the Son of God, why don't You command these stones to be made into bread?" (Matt. 4:3.) There must have been some stones nearby which looked like loaves of bread. A man, who was exceedingly hungry, could look with great longing at a pile of bread-shaped stones and be tempted to go over and grab one and try to devour it. Jesus wasn't moved by Satan's words. The only thing that moved the Lord was the voice of the One who thundered from heaven.

Desires Can Trip You Up

Before we go any further, I want to draw your attention to the phrase the devil used when he tempted Jesus. He said, "*If* You are the Son of God" (Luke 4:3). Satan knew who Jesus Christ was. In Ezekiel 28:14 the Bible says that Lucifer, who was later called Satan, was the covering angel, the one who covered the very person of the Almighty. He was the most magnificent and brightest of all the archangels. He was present in the beginning when the morning stars sprang from the darkness. He knew Jesus Christ when Jesus, the Father, and the Holy Spirit created the world and made man.

Satan was having a memory lapse. He said, "*If* You are the Son of God." The devil always comes to sow doubt in your mind about who Jesus is, what He said, and what He has done. Remember, Satan is a liar and the father of lies. (John 8:44.) Don't you dare believe him when he tells you that the Lord hasn't really healed you. Don't believe him when he tells you that the seed you've sown is money cast into the wind or that you are serving God for nothing.

Satan taunted Jesus, "*If* You really are the Son of God, why don't You command these stones to be turned into piping-hot loaves of bread?" What a temptation for a man who hadn't eaten for forty days and forty nights.

The devil came at Jesus' flesh—at His weakest point. I've got news for you. If Satan came against the flesh and the weaknesses of Jesus, he will come against your flesh and your weaknesses, too. Satan will do everything in his power to try to get you in the flesh. There are many people today who love God; yet they have fallen prey to the temptations of their flesh and have slipped and fallen into sin.

David's Sin

Look at the story of King David in 2 Samuel 11. Here was a man after God's own heart, and yet Satan caught him at the point of his weakness—his flesh—and he fell into sin. One sultry night when David should have been out on the battlefield with his soldiers marching against the enemies of Israel, he decided to stay behind at the palace. What a fateful decision.

The king was restless, pacing back and forth on the roof, when suddenly he noticed a lovely woman bathing nearby. Instead of showing respect for her privacy by turning away, he watched her and lusted after her. Then, in the heat of passion, he took things one step further and sent for her.

After they had spent the night together, Bathsheba became pregnant. David was so terrified that his evil deed would be discovered that he tried to trick Bathsheba's husband, Uriah, into coming back from the battlefield and sleeping with her himself, but he refused. So David sent him into the thick of the battle where he knew Uriah would be killed.

After Uriah's death, the prophet Nathan confronted David with his sin. The great king of Israel repented before God, but he still paid a terrible price when Bathsheba's baby died. (2 Sam. 12:13,16.)

Satan will come against your flesh. He'll tell you, "It's all right to sleep with her or him just this once." Or he'll tell you, "If you go ahead and have that affair, you can have that relationship you've been longing for." Or he'll whisper in your ear, "If you'll just take this drug or satisfy this particular area of your life or go to this Web site or call this 900 number, you can satisfy your flesh."

How did Jesus overcome Satan's temptation against His flesh? He said, "It is written, 'Man shall not live by bread alone [or man shall not live by his flesh], but by every word of God'" (Luke 4:4). Jesus was saying, "We must live by what God says." I want you to notice that He didn't say we should live by *half* the words that God speaks, but by *every* word that proceeds out of the mouth of God.

Let me draw your attention to the fact that Jesus never spoke His own words to Satan. He never tried to match wits with the devil or try to take Satan on in His humanity. He used that which is eternal—the Word of God, the sword of the Spirit. He said, "It is written." The Word of God cuts Satan like a knife.

When the devil launches an attack against me, I don't sit down and have a conversation with him. I don't try to reason with him or try to analyze and figure out his strategy. I do what Jesus did. I quote the Word of God to him, because God's Word can blast a hole in the devil's eardrums.

When Satan comes against your flesh, tell him, "It is written," and begin to quote the Scriptures out loud to him. You're not only driving him away from your flesh by the Word, but you're also building up your faith, for "...faith comes by hearing, and hearing by the word of God" (Rom. 10:17). The most precious words you can ever hear or say are the words of God Almighty.

Guard Your Heart

You would think by this time that the devil would have had enough, but anybody who contends with the Almighty isn't all there anyway. Satan took Jesus up into an exceedingly high mountain and showed Him all the kingdoms of this world and their wealth and glory. Then he said, "I'll give You all this power and splendor if You'll only bow down and worship me." (Luke 4:5-7.)

Just picture for a moment all the glory of this earth, all the glittering cities, the capitals of the nations, the reigning kings and rulers, the great masses of population, the gold and silver, the diamonds on the fingers of the wealthy ladies and gentlemen, the hidden treasures, the fine parades, all the wonders of the world displayed in a moment of time.

Remember, Jesus' divine destiny was to rule over the kingdoms of this earth. He knew that was part of His ultimate mission. The devil whispered slyly, "Jesus, You're at the threshold of the most anointed ministry the world has ever known. I have something to give You that's befitting Your great mission. You've wanted it ever since You were a little boy, and all You have to do to get it is bow down to me."

Satan came against Jesus through His desires, and he comes against you and me in exactly the same way. You may be thinking, *Doesn't the Bible say that God will give me the desires of my heart?* (Ps. 37:4.) It does, but it does not say that He will give you the desires of your mind. Yes, Satan will show you what you can have if you will only allow your mind to rule over your spirit. God created us to keep our minds in subjection to our spirits. (2 Cor. 10:5.)

Satan will try to pervert your God-given desires. He'll lay out before you everything you can have if you will only bow down and worship him. His temptations are being paraded on every street corner. They bombard you through many of the movies Hollywood makes. They entice you through certain Web sites on the Internet. There's no short-age of the availability of sin.

How did Jesus handle this temptation? He told Satan, "For it is written, 'You shall worship the Lord your God, and Him only you shall serve'" (Luke 4:8). He was really saying, "Devil, I'm going to get My desires met in the right way." The Son of God took the Word of God and said, "Devil, it is written." He repulsed Satan, defeated him, and whipped him by using God's Word. You and I can do the same thing when we speak God's Word aloud for the devil to hear.

Guard Against Pride

Before Jesus was tempted in the wilderness, He had just had a tremendous peak experience with His heavenly Father. The God of all creation had sent a powerful sign to confirm Jesus' ministry. After being baptized in the Jordan River, the Lord waded out of the water, the heavens opened, the Spirit of the Lord descended upon Jesus in a form like a dove, and an audible voice thundered from above, saying, "This is My beloved Son, in whom I am well pleased" (Matt. 3:17).

You talk about success. The Most High God had given Jesus Christ His own personal endorsement. What if God the Father told everybody how great you were? What if He sent the Holy Spirit to light upon your head in the form of a dove? What if He told the whole world that you were His beloved son and He was well pleased with you? You'd probably be tempted to get a big head and think that you were the most impor-tant person in the world, wouldn't you?

Carefully read this next statement. After you've experienced an out-standing success, the tempter will come. He'll try to sell you on yourself. He will tell you that you don't need God's help anymore. I believe you have to guard yourself more after you've experienced success than when you've experienced a shattering setback. After a success, the devil tells you,

"Look what you did. No one can defeat you now." Watch out. Proverbs 16:18 says, "Pride goes before destruction, and a haughty spirit before a fall." And Proverbs 13:10 tells us, "By pride comes nothing but strife."

Immediately afterwards, Satan took Jesus away to the pinnacle of the temple and began to bombard Him with more temptations.

There's something else I want to point out to you about the devil's tactics. When he heard Jesus say, "It is written," he thought to himself, *Now that's a good line. I ought to use that line myself.* With this temptation Satan began to mimic the Lord.

Jesus had quoted Scriptures to the devil, so Satan turned around and quoted Scriptures back to Him. He said, "If You are the Son of God, throw Yourself down from here. For it is written: 'He shall give His angels charge over you, to keep you,' and, 'In their hands they shall bear you up, lest [at any time] you dash your foot against a stone'" (Luke 4:9-11).

Turn in your Bible to Psalm 91:11-12 and read the passage Satan was referring to. Notice that in the *King James Version* of Luke 4:11 Satan tucked in three extra words—at any time—which were not in the original text.

This Scripture in the Psalms actually says, "For he shall give his angels charge over you, to keep you in all your ways. In their hands they shall bear you up, lest you dash your foot against a stone." It does *not* say "lest *at any time* you dash your foot against a stone." In other words, God isn't saying that any time you jump off the top of a building, He will send His angels to catch you in their arms. That would be tempting the Lord, and that's not what this Scripture is talking about.

We can never falsify a Scripture, take it out of context, or misapply it and think that it will work. It will not. God is not obligated to perform His Word when it has been misapplied, falsified, or imitated.

Satan mimicked Jesus by quoting Scriptures back to Him, but he misquoted the Word of God. Jesus cut through the devil's lies when He replied, "It has been said, 'You shall not tempt the Lord your God'" (Luke 4:12). He was saying, "Lucifer, you were up in heaven with Me in the beginning. You tried to tempt God back then, but you didn't get away with it. When you stood up and tried to exalt yourself above the throne of majesty, you know what happened. The Lord gave you a swift kick and smashed you down to the earth, and you've been a basket case ever since."

It's important for you to realize that Satan loves to take a portion of the Word of God and quote it to you and make it sound right. It will appeal to your pride. You'll say, "I remember reading that verse in the book of Psalms. It must be right." No, Satan is perverting the Scripture. He's attacking you in the same area he attacked Jesus: pride.

What does pride do in your life? It causes you to make wrong decisions and say things you will later regret. Satan said to Jesus, "Throw Yourself down from the top of the temple. God will protect You." You see, your pride says, "This sin won't really destroy me. I can get away with it just this once. I can take it right up to the edge, and it will be all right." There are many Christians today who are living on the edge, and they don't realize that they're about to slip over because of their pride. Your pride can cost you everything.

I remember my father telling the story of a beautiful woman with flaming red hair who came in the prayer line at one of his crusades. She was an opera singer who had lost her voice, and it had cut off her ability to earn her living as a singer.

Many people knew who this woman was. When she came into the prayer line, the Holy Spirit revealed to my dad that she was dealing with a pride issue. My father said to her, "Ma'am, I want you to run up and down the center aisle seven times as a point of contact for God to heal your voice." Immediately she bristled, stuck her nose up in the air, turned around, and walked off. My dad just shrugged his shoulders and kept praying for the rest of the people in the prayer line.

A few minutes later he looked up and saw this woman running down the center aisle toward him, her hands in the air and tears streaming down her face. She turned around and ran back again. Seven times she repeated the process, and afterward she let out a joyous shout. God had completely healed her. Why? Because she had dealt with the pride issue. She had laid her pride at the feet of Jesus.

How To Handle Pride

When Satan misquoted Scripture, Jesus answered him once again with the Word of God. He quoted Deuteronomy 6:16, saying, "You shall not tempt the Lord your God...." In other words, He was saying, "You shall not be a prideful person." It's important for you to eliminate pride, or it will destroy you.

The Lord Jesus Christ dealt with the pride issue by quoting the Word of God. Notice that He began His encounter with the devil by quoting the Scriptures, He continued by quoting the Scriptures, and He ended His dealings with Satan by quoting God's Word. What does the Bible say happened to Jesus after He quoted the Word of God to the devil? It says, "Then the devil left Him, and behold, angels came and ministered to Him" (Matt. 4:11).

No one is exempt from Satan's attack. He's going to come against your flesh, your pride, and your desires in the same way that he came against the Lord Jesus. If you will do what Jesus did, you can overcome the devil in the same way.

The next time Satan tries to get his hooks into you, just tell him, "Satan, it is written that I'm a blood-bought, blood-washed child of God. It may seem as though my hope is gone, but it's not, because the Word of God says that I overcome by the blood of the Lamb and by the Word of my testimony. (Rev. 12:11.) Take that, devil, in Jesus' name."

Chapter 5

Never Give Up on Your Miracle

When we give our hearts to the Lord, our spirits become new. We have a new Lord and Master, but it's still the same old world out there and the same old enemy coming against us. We're still going to encounter trials, obstacles, and roadblocks from time to time that can make us feel hopeless. Remember, though, our God is still the same God who can turn bad and worse into miracles.

Take, for example, the life of King David. He was a man who was anointed by the prophet Samuel to be the king of Israel; yet, he encountered many obstacles and stumbling blocks in his life. When he was a young shepherd boy, he went to the battlefield to see his brothers, and he came face to face with a giant named Goliath. (1 Sam. 17.) Things looked bad.

Bad went to worse when all the armies of Israel fearfully crawled into a hole. Their hearts turned to water, their knees knocked together, and they scattered like chickens on the hillsides. David, however, believed that things could go from bad to worse to a miracle. He believed that God is a God who redeems our lives from destruction. He shouted, "Is there not a cause?" (v. 29) and took on the giant in the power of the Lord.

Goliath was a giant who towered over nine feet tall, his armor weighing some two hundred pounds. I can imagine him standing there, with the sun glinting on his shoulders, casting a giant's shadow across the battlefield. Just think about the terror that must have tried to grip David's heart when he stepped onto the battlefield. After all, Goliath was a professional soldier, a mercenary, and David was a teenager. How big do you think that giant must have looked to him?

In the same way, our giants, or our problems, always seem to be big and tall. We fling open the door one morning and there's this great big giant—this gigantic problem—staring us in the face, piling in on top of us. Goliath represents the giants that come against your life and mine. I'm talking about giants of fear, financial ruin, devastating diseases, or a son or daughter who is strung out on drugs or alcohol.

David took on his giant face to face. Instead of buckling under to fear, he ran toward Goliath. He ran toward the problem and met the devil head-on. David believed that when things go from bad to worse, that's the time to expect a miracle.

I can picture the headgear that Goliath must have been wearing—a certain type of helmet with a visor that covered his eyes. I can imagine him flipping up that visor so he could see this little runt of a teenage boy running toward him, not having the slightest idea that David was going to do his battle long distance, and that he was a crack shot with his slingshot.

The young shepherd boy from the hills of Bethlehem swung his slingshot around his head, and the stone whizzed from its socket and smashed into Goliath's forehead. All at once he staggered to the ground, stunned by the force of that blow, and David grabbed the giant's sword and cut off his head. You can imagine what that sight must have looked like as David waved Goliath's head high in the air above the soldiers of Israel.

Suddenly King Saul's men were clamoring around him, patting him on the back, and declaring, "Yeah, we were with you all along." It's so easy for people to jump on the bandwagon and believe God when the miracle is right there in front of them. But I praise God for the man or woman who, when things get bad and then bad turns to worse, stands up and boldly proclaims, "In the name of Jesus, I'm going to believe God."

When Everyone's Against You

Another turning point in David's life came when he and his soldiers returned from a mission and discovered that the Amalekites had plundered the city of Ziklag and burned their homes to the ground. (1 Sam. 30.) It didn't take long for things to go from bad to worse.

When David's men saw the smoldering rubble which had once been their homes, they also discovered that their wives and children had been taken captive. They burst into tears, and the Bible says that they wept so hard they couldn't weep anymore. (v. 4.) Then they became angry and picked up rocks to stone David to death.

When David faced Goliath, he faced an enemy who came at him from the ranks of the Philistines; in other words, an outsider. Now he was facing opposition from within his own ranks. Six hundred of David's own choice men had turned against him. His own leaders were ready to take David's neck in their hands because they had lost it all.

Does that describe you today? Perhaps you feel as if you've lost everything. But notice something. David didn't buy the devil's lie that when things go from bad to worse, they automatically have to go to destruction. He believed that God could turn bad and even worse into a miracle. Here are four powerful steps David took that caused him to receive his miracle:

1. David encouraged himself in the Lord.

It's wonderful when your friends and family shower you with words of encouragement. It's so comforting when you're down-and-out and somebody pats you on the shoulder or hugs your neck and reassures you, saying, "Everything is going to be all right."

What about the times when your friends and family shut you out? What do you do when the ones who are the closest to you stab you in the back? What happens when there's no one around to give you a kind word? You've got to encourage yourself in the Lord.

I'm not talking about giving yourself a nice little pep talk here or about the power of positive thinking, although a great big positive dose of God's Word can do your thinking a world of good. Some people try to encourage themselves by turning to a bottle, to drugs, or to some other form of unhealthy or addictive behavior. Sometimes even Christians try to numb themselves to the pain and trials of life through various unhealthy escape and defense mechanisms. God has provided supernatural encouragement for our souls that far surpasses anything the world has to offer.

When David encouraged himself in the Lord, he must have begun to count his blessings, one by one. He must have thought about the supernatural way God had snatched him from the paws of both a lion and a bear. (1 Sam. 17:37.) He must have reminded himself of how he had triumphed over an uncircumcised giant named Goliath, even though he was a virtually unarmed shepherd boy.

Perhaps David began to sing praise songs unto the Lord. No doubt he began to lift his voice to God in prayer. The Bible doesn't say exactly what he did to encourage himself in the Lord, but the bottom line is this: David let God help him get his spirit man to stand up on the inside.

It's hard to receive a miracle from God when your spirit man is lying down. I'm talking about the real you on the inside. Maybe the devil has knocked the wind out of your sails. Perhaps he has stolen your possessions and robbed you of your family, health, peace, and joy. Before you can recover it all, your spirit man needs to stand up tall. You've got to encourage yourself in the Lord.

2. David inquired of the Lord.

David got hooked up with God's miracle power by inquiring of the Lord. Never forget that you have a Savior you can run to when your hope seems gone.

David asked the Lord, "What shall I do?" When you're blasted by torrents of hell, struck down by cancer, sideswiped by the devil, your body is broken up, and your finances are wiped out, it's time to ask the Lord, "What shall I do?" God has a supernatural plan of deliverance for your life.

David went to the Lord for advice. He said, "Should we pursue this host that has plundered our city and carried away our wives and children, or should we just forget about the whole thing? Should we let Satan have it all, or should we go after him in the Name of the Lord?" Thank God, the Lord had an answer for him. He said, "Pursue, for you shall surely overtake them and without fail recover it all" (1 Sam. 30:8).

Don't run from the devil. When you feel like doing that, it's time for you to go to the Lord and instead put Satan on the run.

3. David and his men entered into a faith agreement.

Before David set out to recover everything, he recruited some godly men to enter into a faith agreement with him. In Matthew 18:18-19 Jesus declared, "Assuredly, I say to you, whatever you bind on earth will be bound in heaven, and whatever you loose on earth will be loosed in heaven. Again I say to you that if two of you agree on earth concerning anything that they ask, it will be done for them by My Father in heaven."

Don't pass over this Scripture lightly. Jesus said, "Assuredly," or, "I give you My word of assurance." Jesus promised that God, our heavenly Father, would back up our prayers of agreement. When Jesus makes a promise, you can count on it.

Here are five very important principles about the prayer of agreement that can help you receive your deliverance:

a. **A prayer of agreement must be in accordance with the Word of God.**

What you're believing for has got to be in harmony with the Bible. It can't be based on a wish, whim, or vain imagination. Your agreement has to be with God and His Word.

b. **You need to know with whom you're going into agreement.**

Don't run to someone you hardly know and ask them, "Will you agree with me about this?" Pray, "Heavenly Father, in the name of Jesus, show me specifically who You want me to go into agreement with." I believe God will reveal that person to you.

I'm very careful about who I share my prayer requests with because I don't want to give Satan a chance to destroy my prayer of agreement. The Bible tells us in 2 Corinthians 6:14 not to be unequally yoked together with unbelievers. If someone's faith isn't in agreement with yours and they don't believe the same things about God's Word that you believe, how can they enter into agreement with you?

Your faith can be built up high and you can be standing on God's Word, but if you ask someone to agree with you who doesn't believe that part of the Word, they can dash your faith to pieces. They can wipe out all the power of your agreement by their unbelief. It's important to find someone of like faith to agree with you.

c. **Know what you are agreeing on.**

The Bible teaches us to be specific with the Lord. Philippians 4:6 says, "Let your requests be made known to God." Isaiah 43:26 tells us, "Put Me in remembrance; Let us contend together; State your case, that you may be acquitted."

Plead your case before God. Tell Him specifically what you need. Remind Him of what His Word says about your needs, and make certain that whomever you're asking to agree with you understands exactly what you're agreeing for. If both of you are not believing for the same thing, it's hard for the prayer of agreement to work.

d. Before you go into agreement with someone, ask yourself these questions: What am I permitting in my life? What am I to stop in my life?

The *Today's English Version* says, "What you prohibit [or stop] on earth will be prohibited [or stopped] in heaven, and what you permit on earth will be permitted in heaven" (Matt. 18:18).

Many times we desire the will of God, but our actions can stop it from happening. Other times we don't want certain bad things to happen, but our actions can permit them to happen. Another way to put it is this: Whatever you allow, God allows.

Maybe you're allowing things in your life that are against God. Until you bind those things and remove them from your life, the path between you and your miracle will always be filled with traps and land mines. In other words, you've got to get rid of the junk.

e. Once you enter into an agreement, don't come out of it.

Stick to it. It's like a legal contract. Before you enter into a legal contract, you carefully examine the fine print. You make certain that both parties are in harmony, because once that contract is signed, it becomes a binding agreement. It's the same way with the Word of God. Once you come into agreement with God's Word for a miracle, don't come out of the agreement until the miracle comes.

A lot of people say, "Oh, yeah, I'll agree with you." And then they walk right out the door and exclaim, "God, I wonder," and they cancel out the agreement by their doubt and unbelief. Or suddenly the circumstances change, and poof, all of their faith goes up in smoke.

When you go into a prayer of agreement, you're bound by God's Word to stick to that agreement regardless of the circumstances. If the outward circumstances frighten somebody, then they're not the right person for you to go into agreement with.

I encourage you to find what you're believing for in the Word of God and then don't budge. You've got to have pit bull faith. Get hold of God's promise, grit your teeth, and don't be moved by your feelings or the circumstances. That's the kind of agreement that can produce miracles.

4. David finished the fight.

Questions plague the minds of many Christians when their lives seem to be blasted to smithereens. Many times they don't feel like going on. Jesus told us in Luke 9:62 to keep our hands on the plow.

Revelation 3:21 also tells us that Jesus had to overcome, and we have to overcome too. If you never experience any difficulties in life, there's no way you can be an overcomer in Christ. Have you ever stopped to think that your level of victory is not determined by how big or how bad the devil's attack is? It's how you respond to his attack with your faith. You've got to fight the good fight of faith until you win.

Many times Christianity is preached as a surface religion. People get the mistaken notion that you can give your heart to Jesus, and then your life will be all peaches and cream. They don't realize there is a devil on the loose on planet earth. There are opposing forces that don't want us to serve God and will do everything they can to steal our hope in God.

When Lindsay and I lost our son, Richard Oral, after only thirty-six hours of life, we felt as if our insides were being ripped to pieces. Like David and his men, we wept until we couldn't weep anymore. Thank God, we serve a God who doesn't leave us standing in the dust, with our lives shattered, crying our insides out. He provides supernatural help for us to recover all.

Not only did God lift us out of our despair, but He also helped us try again. Satan had told Lindsay and me that we would never have children; then he snuffed out the life of our firstborn. The devil doesn't play fair, but remember, Satan never catches the Lord off guard.

Satan may have shaken us to the very core of our being when he snatched away the life of our precious son, but God didn't fall off the throne when this happened. He had a plan for us to recover all. Lindsay and I locked hands with the Lord and began to press forward in faith. God has given us three beautiful daughters. No, they can never take the place of the child we lost, but God gave us the strength to fight the enemy of our soul until we won.

David and his men could have collapsed in the middle of that heap of smoking ashes at Ziklag; instead, they chose to fight. They fought their enemies until they won. They crushed the Amalekites, and 1 Samuel 30:19 says that David recovered all that they had carried away. *The Amplified Bible* says, "Nothing was missing, small or great, sons or daughters, spoil or anything that had been taken; David recovered all. Also David captured all the flocks and herds [which the enemy had], and the people drove those animals before him and said, This is David's spoil" (1 Sam. 30:19,20).

Isn't that the way you want to return home from your battles with satanic forces? Not only can you recover everything the devil has stolen from you, but you can also march home from the battle loaded down with the spoils of his kingdom. That is God's victorious plan for your life.

Chapter 6

Surviving in a Crazy, Mixed-up World

My wife Lindsay's family is a living testimony of the fact that you can survive emotionally in a crazy, mixed-up world.

When Lindsay was twelve years old, her father was struck down by cancer. He was in the prime of his life, a young father with a beautiful wife and three young children, and the youngest president of the Automotive Dealers Association of America. He was suddenly snatched away from them by cancer. I've asked Lindsay to tell you the story in her own words:

When I was twelve years old my father was diagnosed with acute leukemia, and the doctors said that he would die within six months. My family had been in church all of our lives, but we didn't know that we could speak healing to our father and that he could live and not die. We didn't know Jesus had said that we could have whatsoever we said. (Mark 11:23,24.)

We went around telling everybody, "Our father is going to die in six months," and sadly, he beat our predictions. He died five months and two days later.

I remember walking into my father's hospital room one day shortly before he died, and he was talking to someone on the telephone. He whispered to me that Oral Roberts was on the other end of the line.

At first I thought he was kidding. My dad was always laughing and telling jokes. His name was Harry, and everybody called him Happy Harry because he was so jovial. When he told me that Oral Roberts was on the phone, I said, "Ha, ha, that's very funny."

"No, it really is Oral Roberts," he insisted.

"No, it's not." I replied emphatically. But it really was Oral Roberts on the other end of the line that day. One of my dad's friends knew Lee Braxton, who

was one of Oral's right-hand men, and Lee had asked Oral to pray for my dad. Thank God, Oral cared enough to call and pray.

My father still died. He went on to be with the Lord painlessly. My mother and I believe that when Oral called, my father gave his life to Jesus. My family never forgot how he picked up the telephone and prayed for my dad.

My mother had been a partner with Oral Roberts Ministries for years, and she faithfully planted her seeds of faith to God. I remember one time when she read an article that blasted Oral Roberts, saying he took money from widows. My mother looked at that article and exclaimed, "This isn't right. I'm one of those widows. If it hadn't been for Oral Roberts teaching me about seedtime and harvest, we would have starved to death."

When my father died, our means of support died too. We had never suffered from lack of anything when my father was alive. As soon as he died, we lost almost all that we had overnight. I remember telling my mother one time when she was sowing a seed to God, "Mother, you can't afford to sow that kind of seed."

She just looked at me and said, "I can't afford not to sow it." And she meant it.

It wasn't long after my father died that my mother was diagnosed with an ovarian cyst, and our family felt as though our hope had vanished. Thank God, my mother survived the surgery. Later, our family moved from Michigan to Florida, and we continued our partnership with Oral Roberts Ministries. Oral had just written a book called "3 Most Important Steps to Your Better Health and Miracle Living." He sent my mother a copy of that book, and after we had read it, we began to think and talk differently. We began to find things in the Scriptures that we didn't even know were there. And we began to believe God for healing.

Then Satan attacked my mother's lungs, and the doctors thought it was cancer. I remember one time when my mother went for an x-ray. She was sitting in a chair in the waiting area afterward, when all at once she felt a burning hot hand touch her right side. She turned around, but nobody was there. She felt that heat burn all the way through her lungs.

The doctor had already seen the bad report on the x-rays, but my mother insisted, "Let's take one more x-ray." He agreed, so they took another x-ray, and then they took a series of x-rays. The doctor kept saying, "Let's just watch it." That was over twenty-five years ago, and they're still watching it. After all of these years, my mother is the picture of health, and God is being glorified.

I wonder what would have happened if Lindsay's mother had decided to have a pity party instead of sowing her seeds to God for her healing. Lindsay and her family had plenty of reasons to feel as if life had dealt them a cruel blow. It had. They could have caved in emotionally and become bitter, blaming God for letting their husband and father die. They could have let that tragedy leave them emotionally crippled.

Do you realize that if Lindsay and her mother had clung to their past and nursed their wounds, Lindsay might never have become my wife? She might never have fulfilled her destiny to become a minister of the Gospel to hurting people everywhere.

There comes a time when we have to lay down the past. Isaiah 43:18-19 declares, "Do not remember the former things, nor consider the things of old. Behold, I will do a new thing, now it shall spring forth; shall you not know it? I will even make a road in the wilderness and rivers in the desert."

You can expect God to do a new thing in your life every day if you need Him to. He had to give Lindsay and her family a new beginning many times. He will do the same thing for you, because He is no respecter of persons.

No Long Distance Relationships

Have you ever wondered how Joseph survived in his crazy, mixed-up world? How did he retain his sanity? He sought a close, personal relationship with God. He didn't have a long distance relationship with the Lord. Many people know about God, but they don't let Him take an active role in their lives unless their back is up against the wall or they're struck by a gut-wrenching tragedy.

In the middle of the hustle-bustle of your daily life, don't miss hearing the still, small voice of the Lord. Don't let the devil quench the fire of God's Spirit in your soul. It's so important to keep your relationship with God up close and personal. When you don't, it's easy for the devil to come in with a flood of adversity that tries to steal your hope. Joseph had a close, personal relationship with God. No matter how bad things got, he found grace to help him in his time of need. The reason he found God's grace and favor was because he was looking for them. Jesus said in Matthew 7:7, "...seek, and you will find; knock, and it will be opened to you."

Joseph was looking for God's grace, and the Lord was with him. He was serving God, loving Him, praising Him, listening to His voice, and searching for His will for his life. He declared, "I may be a slave in jail, but I love You, God, with all of my heart, soul, mind, and strength." Do you love God with everything that's within you? Or do you love Him half-heartedly? Have you totally sold out to the Lord? Do you love Him with reckless abandon? Joseph was sold out to God—lock, stock, and barrel.

A Sense of Purpose

Joseph also had a strong sense of purpose and destiny in his life. Remember, he had two dreams, and his brothers hated him because of his life's vision and his sense of purpose.

Let's examine Joseph's first dream for a moment. He said, "Brothers, I saw you and me out working in the field, binding sheaves." I tell you, if God has put a vision in your heart, it ought to include work. W-O-R-K. James 2:17 declares that "...faith by itself, if it does not have works, is dead." I thank God for faith, but I thank God for the times when you get up off your chair and do something about your faith.

Don't just try to glide through life. Don't be satisfied with mediocrity. Strive for God's best. Give it your all. Joseph was an excellent worker. That's how he achieved such a high position in Potiphar's house. I've got news. God is an excellent God, and He raised you up to be His excellent child, to be a person of excellence and a person of work.

Joseph had a second dream in which he saw the sun, moon, and eleven stars bow down to him, representing his father, mother, and brothers. (Gen. 37:9.) This second vision showed Joseph his purpose, his mission in life—to be a great leader of his people.

Even while he was in prison, Joseph still maintained the vision and mission he received from God. There was no way his life could be over because his dream hadn't come to pass.

Has God placed a dream or a vision in your heart, but with all the commotion that's going on around you, you're wondering, *How can this ever come to pass? Is the box too tight? Are the walls too high? Is the time too short?* No. If the vision has not come to pass, it's not over yet.

Don't Get Bitter, Get Better

Throughout his ordeal, Joseph refused to let people make him bitter; he let them make him better. Joseph would not let anyone make him bitter. He would not allow the actions of others to determine his attitude. It's been said that your attitude in life determines your altitude. That's because if you allow bitterness or a negative attitude to pollute your mind, it's going to drag you down. If you keep your attitude focused on the Lord, you're always going to rise to the top.

You may ask, "But what can I do about this person? I've cried, I've prayed, I've wrestled, I've cast out, I've cast up, and I've cast down. I've been standing here casting and casting, but nothing seems to help." I've got the answer for you: Give that person to God. Say, "Lord, I release this person to You. I can no longer carry them. They're all Yours. I don't have them anymore."

You say, "Well, Richard, that sounds so simple." Much of life is simple if we'll just do what God's Word teaches.

Joseph could have let anger and resentment toward his brothers get down into his spirit. He could have let a bad attitude creep in when Potiphar's wife lied about him and had him cast into prison. He could have gotten bitter when the chief cupbearer didn't tell Pharaoh about him. But Joseph just kept on keeping on. He kept on seeking the Lord and trusting in his God.

One day Pharaoh dreamed a dream that none of his wise men could interpret. (Gen. 41:1-8.) They couldn't get the right mixture of animal entrails spread out on a little dish. That was one of the ways magicians interpreted dreams in those days.

The chief butler remembered a young Jewish man in prison who had interpreted his dream, so Pharaoh quickly had Joseph brought to him from prison. This tells me that when one door shuts, you can expect God to open another door in your life. The new door may be different from the one you thought it would be. You've got to stop trying to figure everything out. Just trust God to open the right door.

God opened the door to Pharaoh's palace for Joseph, and he walked through it. He interpreted Pharaoh's dream.

Later, when famine struck the land of Canaan, Joseph's father sent his sons to Egypt to get some food. (Gen. 42:1-3.) As his brothers bowed before him that day, no doubt Joseph remembered his dream about his brothers' sheaves bowing down to his sheaf. The dream wasn't being fulfilled in exactly the way he had pictured, but it was being fulfilled nonetheless.

No matter what's happening to you right now, remember that God isn't lost and neither are you. You're not out in some vast, uncharted territory like Star Trek. God knows where you are and where you're going, because He has the road map of life.

You may have had a rough childhood and were considered the outcast in your family. You don't have to hold on to the things that happened to you anymore. Let go of your troubled past and expect God to send you on a brand-new journey in your life.

Chapter 7

How It All Began

Oral Roberts University is a fully accredited charismatic university, with five thousand undergraduate and graduate students and nearly forty thousand alumni. It was birthed as a dream in the heart of a stuttering seventeen-year-old boy named Oral Roberts as he lay dying in the backseat of a borrowed car, coughing and hemorrhaging his life away from tuberculosis. The papers had already been signed for him to be admitted to a sanitarium in Talihina, Oklahoma. But that night he was on his way to a healing service in Pontotoc County, Oklahoma, where a man of God was praying for the sick and people were being healed from every type of sickness and disease.

As he rode along in that car, my father could hear the voices of my Uncle Elmer and my grandmother, Claudius Priscilla Roberts, talking through the darkness. They were talking about the many people who had been healed by the power of God that week in the revival.

My dad heard another voice whispering in his ear that night, the voice of almighty God, saying to him, "Son, I am going to heal you, and you are to take My healing power to your generation. And someday you are to build Me a university."

At the close of that healing meeting, my father's stuttering tongue was healed and the tuberculosis was driven from his body through the prayers of an evangelist who believed God could do anything. Raised up from his deathbed, my father was called to preach. That night a spark was ignited in his heart to build God a university based upon His authority and the power of the Holy Spirit. All through the years of the great tent healing campaigns my father conducted, he held on to that dream.

As the years flew by, something like a magnet kept drawing my dad to a choice piece of ground in south Tulsa, Oklahoma. My mind flashes back to the times when I was a boy, and we would drive along Lewis Avenue until we came to a stop in front of that piece of property. My father believed that God had preserved that land for a holy cause—so that a great university might be raised up to the glory of God.

Many years after God spoke to a boy named Oral Roberts in the backseat of a borrowed car, there was another boy whose story is inextricably woven into the fabric of Oral Roberts University—a boy who roamed this piece of ground where ORU now stands, carrying a fishing pole and a baseball bat, a boy without a care in the world. If you let him play all day long, he was happy. He was in his own little world. He was a lot like young David in the Bible...a boy who nobody thought would amount to much.

I'm sure you recall the remarkable story of David. God had commanded the prophet Samuel to anoint a new king over the nation of Israel. Samuel journeyed to Bethlehem, to the house of Jesse, searching for a successor to the throne. As each one of Jesse's sons passed by Samuel, he exclaimed, "No, he's not the one." You see, David had completely slipped everybody's mind, but he was the one God had chosen to be king. (1 Sam. 16:1-13.)

That's also the story of my life. I was the "David" in my family. I was that little boy with a bat, a ball, and a fishing pole, walking home from school with my shirttail torn and dirty, swinging my lunch pail, and whistling a song I'd made up. Everybody thought it would be my older brother who would preach the Gospel.

Build Me a University

As a young man, I was walking down the wrong road, rebellious to my parents and irreverent to the Lord. There was a huge wall that loomed between my dad and me. I'll never forget the summer he wrote to me while I was at Interlochen National Music Camp in Traverse City, Michigan. He told me that God had spoken to him again about Oral Roberts University. The Lord's words to my father were: "Raise up your students to hear My voice, to go where My light is dim, where My voice is heard small, and My healing power is not known…even to the uttermost bounds of the earth. Their work will exceed yours and in this I am well pleased."

My father launched out to build a university during a dangerous time in the U.S. It was in the middle of the violent sixties, when the civil rights movement was in full swing and racial tensions had reached a feverish pitch. It was at the height of the hippie movement, when young people were defying authority and disrupting society in a violent way. There was a restless anti-establishment atmosphere in our country, with the protests raging against the Vietnam War. Crowds were marching in the streets. American flags were being flung to the ground and burned. The National Guard was gunning down student protesters on university campuses. It was an unpredictable time to build a university with a prayer tower as its centerpiece and to boldly proclaim that above all the books of academic learning, the number one book is the Holy Bible.

It was a dangerous time in my life too. Even though I was raised on the Bible, I was not a Christian. I was caught up in the growing tide of rebellion that was sweeping America's youth. I was a runaway from God as well as from my parents. I was having the time of my life, involved in just about everything a teenager could try. In the spring of 1967, I came home from the out-of-state university I was attending for ORU's dedication. I'll never forget how jolted I was by the words Billy Graham spoke that day, just a few months before my nineteenth birthday. He declared, "If this institution ever moves away from faith in the Bible, faith in God, and putting God first, then let us this day pronounce a curse on it." I've never been able to get away from those words.

Later, his words kept ringing in my heart until I finally obeyed the voice of the Lord when He told me that I was supposed to be a student at ORU. After I transferred here, I can remember watching in amazement as some of my dad's Partners pulled into the parking lot in front of Claudius Roberts Dormitory, climbed out of their car on a scorching-hot, 100-degree day, and, with tears rolling down their cheeks, stooped down and kissed the pavement. Then I heard one of them say, "Oh, I can feel Jesus on these grounds." That experience is forever branded in my spirit. It wasn't long—only a matter of a few weeks—before I gave my heart to the Lord.

The Flaming Arrows of the Enemy

Throughout the years, it seems as if the devil has singled out Oral Roberts University, blasting us with his entire arsenal from hell. Why? Because this place is dangerous to Satan. It's hazardous to his health. But even more than that, ORU is precious. It's precious to God and also to the body of Christ. After all, where else are you going to find a fully accredited, academically outstanding, charismatic, Bible-believing university with both undergraduate and graduate schools, where young people can "get a quality education in a Holy Spirit environment" and learn how to hear God's voice?

Yes, there are many other first-rate, Bible-believing Christian colleges throughout this nation and around the world, and I praise God for them. But ORU is special. Even our detractors admit there's no other place in the world like this place. Academics, Holy Ghost prayer, and healthy physical education and aerobics, all in one university.

It was no great surprise to me when Satan launched an all-out assault against ORU in the summer of 1993. Back in the 80s a series of scandals struck the body of Christ. Donations to Oral Roberts University and our ministry dropped by 50 percent in only 30 days. We were not alone. Ministries and churches across the nation had similar experiences. As a result, many Christian schools and churches were struggling. Many ministries simply could not withstand the brutal financial pressure. For the first time ever, ORU and our ministry began a downward spiral into debt. We were hurting. You can imagine how it would feel if your income plummeted by 50 percent without warning. We felt as if the props had been knocked out from under us.

Before that time, there had been no significant debt against ORU or our ministry. Between 1987 and 1993, we tightened our belt, cut a number of programs, and significantly reduced the size of our staff. We were working to be the very best stewards of God's money that we could be. Yet we were floundering, and the debt kept growing.

By the time my father, Oral Roberts, officially stepped down as President and Chief Executive Officer of Oral Roberts University in January 1993, our debt had skyrocketed to $56 million, which is a very large amount of money. It's not such a staggering figure when you consider our debt-to-asset ratio. However, it was still a debt of $56 million, and we had no earthly way of paying it. My father did everything in his power to remove it. It was his desire that all the indebtedness against ORU would be wiped out by the end of his thirty years of tenure. He told me, "Richard, I want you to start with a clean slate." It was certainly a worthy dream, but somehow it was just beyond our fingertips. It nearly broke his heart when he stepped down as president that I was suddenly saddled with it.

When my father announced to the Board of Regents that he would not stand for reelection, he told them, "I recommend my son, Richard, to be your new president, but it's your decision." No one knew who the board's choice would be because they are an autonomous group. They were free to elect whomever they chose. When the appointed time came, the Chairman of the Board, Marilyn Hickey, a dear woman of God, opened the floor for nominations, and my name was placed into nomination. The nominations were then closed.

I wanted to "shoot straight" with the board right from the start, so I asked the chairman if I could say a word before they voted. "If you're casting your vote for me because I'm Oral Roberts' son, I do not wish to be president of this university," I said. "However, if you believe I'm God's man for the job, then I want to be your next president." The vote was cast, and it was unanimous in my favor. We marched across the campus to Christ's Chapel for an installation service before the entire faculty, staff, and student body. I accepted my new position with fear and trepidation—not in the sense of being terrified by it, but in holy fear and reverence for the Lord.

The newspapers flashed the headlines the next day: "The Torch is Passed." After they hung a big medallion around my neck, they handed me the $56 million debt. Do you know what it feels like to owe $56 million? I certainly hope not. However, it's not much different from owing $52,000 or $5,200 if you don't have the money to pay it. You can put the decimal point anywhere you want, debt is still debt.

My father had already told me, "Richard, when I step down as president, your mother and I are going to stay out of the picture as much as possible. I've been ORU's leader for so long that people will try to get around you to get to me. Out of respect for you as the new leader, your mother and I will no longer be active in the university's operations, but I will be available if you need me."

Although I thought I was prepared, nothing quite prepares you to be the president of a university with debt. Almost overnight the fires of hell began licking at my heels. Some of the people who I thought were *for* the university suddenly turned their backs on us. It wasn't long before a whole host of others came crawling out of the woodwork, offering me every scheme and enticement you can possibly imagine.

They would say, "Richard, you're the president now. If you'll just make a few minor changes, we'll support ORU. If you'll stop having Spirit-filled chapel services and shut down the Prayer Tower, we'll send you donations. If you'll take the power of the Holy Spirit out of the university, we'll pour the money in." The forces of hell came at me from every quarter. I was assured a way out from under the debt if I would only compromise what God had called the university to be. The way you spell hell is c-o-m-p-r-o-m-i-s-e.

Thrown Into the Fiery Furnace

Can you imagine the temptation I faced? I understood what Shadrach, Meshach, and Abednego must have experienced when they faced Nebuchadnezzar's burning fiery furnace, which the king heated seven times hotter than ordinary for their punishment. (Dan. 3.) It felt as though the fires of the furnace were heated seven times hotter in my life as well.

If you recall the story, Shadrach, Meshach, and Abednego were among the young Hebrew men and women who were taken captive to Babylon by King Nebuchadnezzar's legions. I want you to picture them as all of a sudden the air was filled with the sound of trumpets, flutes, cornets, and a variety of other musical instruments. Every Babylonian bowed on their faces and began to chant, "Great is Nebuchadnezzar our god. Great is Nebuchadnezzar our god."

The king had a statue of himself made of pure gold. When the music played, everyone in the land had to bow down and worship the image. Anyone who refuses to do so will be thrown into a flaming, fiery furnace.

When Shadrach, Meshach, and Abednego heard Nebuchadnezzar's decree, the blood in their veins turned cold. Their hair stood up on the backs of their necks, but they refused to bow. It didn't take long for the news to reach King Nebuchadnezzar. He called for the three young men and gave them a second chance to bow. Satan will always give you a second chance to turn your back on God. The king declared, "If you bow to my golden image before all of my princes, my governors, my magicians, my family, and my staff, it will go well with you. If you refuse, I'll cast you alive into a burning, fiery furnace. Who is the God that can deliver you out of my hands?"

Those young men looked straight into Nebuchadnezzar's eyes and saw his enraged countenance. They could feel the hot breath of his anger and his furnace heated seven times hotter than ordinary. Shadrach, Meshach, and Abednego didn't budge an inch. They exclaimed, "O king, we don't need to think much on this matter, for our God is able to deliver us, but if not, we will not bow." (vv. 16,17.)

That brings me to two inescapable laws in life. One is the law of faith, which declares that if you don't bow, you won't burn. The other is the law of compromise, which says that if you *do* bow, you will burn. If you serve the Lord, your faith will be tried. If you love God, the world will hate you. If you serve Him with all of your spirit, soul, mind, and strength, all of hell's fury will be unleashed against you. That's why you must not allow it to get in you when you're going through it.

There will always be a Nebuchadnezzar and a fiery furnace. The devil will always make sure an opportunity to compromise is around every corner. You'll find that when you *do* compromise, you'll generally lose what you sought to gain. In other words, compromise costs. Compromise calls from every street corner. The kingpins of this world are clamoring for you to compromise. They'll try to persuade you by saying, "If you don't go along with our plans, you're going to lose your job, you're going to lose your husband or wife, you're going to lose your friends, your family, your business, your financial status. You'll even lose your respect." However, you don't have to yield to their threats.

The Word Is Full of Compromise

Let's get down to the real nuts and bolts of the matter. I recall the story of a pastor who was extremely disillusioned with his ministry. His congregation was dwindling instead of growing, and he was so perplexed by the whole situation that he decided to drive to a nearby city to get away from it all.

The next thing he knew, he found himself in a bar, slumped over on a barstool, clutching a glass of liquor in his hand and sipping it, when all at once he asked himself, "What on earth am I doing here? This is ridiculous." He recounted later, "I slammed the glass down on the bar and got up and walked out the door. I wanted to go home, but I had the smell of liquor on my breath and it would take some time for that smell to go away. I didn't know what else to do, so I drove around for a little while. I passed a movie theater and thought, *I'll go to a movie, and by the time it's over, the liquor smell will be gone and I can go home.*

"As I was standing in line to purchase my ticket," he said, "an attractive young woman walked up and propositioned me. I wasn't paying much attention to her, so I asked her in a flippant sort of way, 'What's the going rate?'

"'Just a minute,' she told me and then disappeared around the corner. Only a few seconds later she reappeared with a policeman on each arm. The next thing I knew, I was under arrest, standing before a judge, facing an arraignment, and wondering, *How on earth did I get myself into this predicament?* A public defender was by my side, and he whispered to me, 'You can plead guilty, or you can plead innocent. If you plead innocent, they'll schedule a trial date.'"

The pastor knew he couldn't afford the scandal of a trial, so he asked the lawyer, "What happens if I plead guilty?"

"You'll have to pay a fine," the public defender responded, "and then you'll be dismissed."

As the pastor stood before the judge, he stated flatly, "Your honor, I really don't know what to say. I'm not guilty of any crime. In an offhanded way, I merely asked the lady, 'What's the going rate?' Actually, it was a case of entrapment, and I'm not guilty. But I'll go ahead and plead guilty and pay the fine."

After paying the fine, he was informed, "By the way, you'll have to report to a parole officer in your hometown once a week." His heart sank the moment he heard those words. It was all over. He knew he was finished.

The poor man drove back home in a daze. As soon as he could, he gathered his church members around him and told them the story from start to finish. Then he groaned, "I'm so sorry that I compromised. Please forgive me. I'm going to resign." His church was so moved by his honesty and repentant heart that they assured him, "No, we don't want you to resign. We need a man like you as our pastor." Do you see how his compromise nearly cost him everything?

How can I describe life's fiery furnaces? It's the story of the young man who makes his sexual pitch to a young lady, and she rolls her eyes at him and says to herself, *He's the best thing that's come down the pike in a long time. I guess I'd better give in, or he'll find somebody else.* As soon as she surrenders to him, she loses respect for herself and for him. Then he walks away, and she feels about two inches tall. He says, "Love me tonight, if only for one night." Six weeks later she is parked all alone in front of an abortion clinic, trying to figure out whether or not she should kill the fetus inside her body. You see, the world is full of compromise.

It Looked Like the End of the Line

Shadrach, Meshach, and Abednego proclaimed, "O king, we may burn in your furnace, but we will not bow to your god." Hell was coming after them with all of its fury, but they refused to let go of their hope. Nebuchadnezzar flew into a rage as he bellowed, "Stoke that furnace seven times hotter than ordinary, and throw the Hebrews into the fire." He called on his mightiest men to throw the young men into the fiery furnace. As they tried to carry out their orders, they were consumed by the flames. You see, they weren't made out of the right kind of stuff.

When the door to the furnace was slammed shut, Nebuchadnezzar whispered to himself, *That's it. It's settled. No one will ever dare to take me on again. The next time the music sounds, everybody will be dancing and everybody will be bowing. They'll be singing my song: "Great is Nebuchadnezzar our god."* The king waited a while and then muttered to himself, *Those ropes ought to be burned up by now, and their clothing is bound to be engulfed in flames. Pretty soon we'll be able to smell their burning flesh.* A few minutes later, Nebuchadnezzar declared, "Open the door." And what he saw made his hair stand on end.

I want you to picture this scene. When Nebuchadnezzar peered into the fire, he saw three young men marching in the middle of the flames and singing praises to their God. The king gasped when he looked in again, for he saw a fourth Man in the midst of the fire, and the fourth Man looked like the Son of God. (v. 25.) At the very instant Nebuchadnezzar had those Hebrews thrown into the flames, Jesus Christ reached across the lap of God the Father and grabbed three Holy Ghost asbestos suits. Then the fourth Man, traversing time and space, catapulted down into the midst of the fire.

Before the flames could begin to lick upon their bodies, He exclaimed, "Brothers, put on these suits. They're divine protection. I'm going to lead you safely through the fire. They started doing a Jericho march in the middle of the flames. They might have been singing, "We bring the sacrifice of praise into the house of the Lord," and jumping, dancing, and praising their God.

When Nebuchadnezzar pulled them out of the furnace, he sniffed their clothing, but there was no smell of smoke upon them. Even their hair and skin were not singed. The king whirled around and proclaimed, "If anybody says anything bad about the God of Shadrach, Meshach, and Abednego, he shall be cut into pieces, for no other God can deliver like this." (v. 29.)

When the three Hebrews refused to compromise and bow to Nebuchadnezzar's golden image, they were thrown into a fiery hell. They escaped unharmed because they refused to let go of their hope and allow hell to get into them.

Standing Strong for God

I know what the roaring flames of the fire look like. Even though at times my hope has waned, I refused to give in to the hell that surrounded me. I've made a Holy Ghost decision that I'm going to stand for what God stands for and stay on track with Him. I've decided to honor the Lord no matter what the cost. You may be facing a battle of your faith today and your hope seems gone, but don't give up. You can make a Holy Ghost decision that the gates of hell are not going to prevail against you. When you take a stand for the Lord, you can expect Him to take a stand for you.

Chapter 8

$56 Million Has a Whole Lot of Zeros

When I assumed the role of President of Oral Roberts University, I felt like the whole world was watching. It seemed as if people all across America were speculating about what Richard Roberts would do next and whether or not I would depart from ORU's founding purpose. The naysayers had prophesied for many years that no one would be able to maintain ORU when my father was no longer active in its administration. They insisted that ORU would fall by the wayside, that it would become a secular university.

The devil tried to show me a day when there would be no Prayer Tower at Oral Roberts University, no Holy Spirit-filled chapel services, no uncompromising stand on the Word of God, and no power of prayer. He tried to show me a day when the faculty would be allowed to run wild and publish anything they wanted to, whether or not it was in harmony with the power of the Holy Spirit and the founding purpose of the university. That thought sent shivers up and down my spine.

Satan bombarded me with images of ORU going the way of many other universities that originally were founded on the power of God, but now they're mere shadows of their beginnings. The devil sneered at me, "It took your father thirty years to build this university, but I'm going to destroy it in one year through you." I awakened in the night from nightmares of newspaper headlines saying everything was going under. In the natural, it looked like Satan was right on target. We were going from pillar to post in our finances. I was making regular trips downtown to see our bankers, and every time I came out of their offices, I felt as if I had blood running down my face because of the ghastly financial beating I was taking. I felt like a fireman because I spent all of my time putting out fires.

By July it seemed as if my life were disintegrating. The weight of the debt was so colossal and overwhelming that I decided God couldn't possibly carry it by Himself, so I tried to help Him. Even though we know that God is God, we sometimes try to shoulder our own load, forgetting the words that Jesus said, "Cast your burden upon Me. I can carry it." (1 Peter 5:7.)

In the meantime, my wife was seeing the change in me. She said that I was angry all the time. My stomach was tied up in knots. I had developed an ulcer. Everything inside me was always churning, and no matter what I did, I couldn't seem to settle down. Resting and sleeping became increasingly difficult. I had become an unholy terror. My attitude had gone down the tubes. The initial happiness and elation I had felt when I was elected president of ORU had turned into a dark scowl. I wanted to run away.

I sought God constantly. I was pacing the floor, crying out in the night, my body shaking in agony. I was calling on the Lord, stretching myself out to Him, desperately grappling with my faith. There were times when I literally put my Bible on the floor and stood on it. By faith, I was standing on the Word of God, believing that He would shatter the devil's blow against Oral Roberts University.

As I cried out to the Lord, He began to draw my attention to several areas of the university where we had somehow gotten off track. Have you ever unraveled a mystery in your life? You had no idea why things were so bad, so topsy-turvy or out of kilter, but suddenly a light bulb flashed on in your mind, and God supernaturally revealed the trouble to you. After the first six months of my tenure as president of Oral Roberts

University, I began to unravel the mystery surrounding why the devourer was not being rebuked on our behalf.

God Never Overlooks Seed

I made a discovery that summer that hit me like a freight train. As we had struggled to pay the mounting bills, somehow in the middle of all the rough financial waters, the decision had been made to cut off our corporate tithing. Lindsay and I had never stopped our personal tithing, but our financial staff had apparently become so concerned with watching every penny that they had completely shut down our ministry's giving to other ministries and works of the Lord.

I understand how tempting it can be to draw back on your giving when you get into a financial bind. However, that is one of the worst things you could possibly do. No wonder we were sinking so fast. ORU and our ministry weren't sowing tithes and offerings to the Lord. The windows of heaven were slammed shut. When you do this, without any warning, you're left standing out in the cold, wondering why your windows of blessing are closed up tight. In the meantime, the devourer (the devil) is not rebuked, and he's running roughshod over your entire life. (Mal. 3:10,11.)

When I realized what had happened, I felt like the Israelites in the book of Malachi when they exclaimed, "Lord, how have we left You?" Did you know that it's possible to slip away from the Lord in a certain area of your life and not even be aware of it? God told Israel, "You've left Me. You've robbed Me," and the people cried in disbelief, "How have we left You? How have we robbed You?" He explained, "You've robbed Me in tithes and offerings." (Mal. 3:8.)

I discovered that we had done the same thing the Israelites had done, even though we had not been aware of it. The instant I uncovered this shattering piece of information, I led ORU and our ministry in a corporate time of repentance before the Lord. Nothing beats a good old-fashioned confession. We made a solemn vow that from that day forward we would tithe off of every dollar that came into our ministry.

I gathered my administrative team together and told them, "I don't care how much it hurts or how impossible it looks in the natural, we're going to give 10 percent of our daily income as tithes to the Lord." They agreed with me 100 percent even though they knew how difficult it would be. Everybody knew that tithing was our only hope of crawling out from under that avalanche of bills. By eleven o'clock in the morning we usually knew what our income for that day was, and every day we faithfully sowed 10 percent to God. We began to sow across the nation and around the world.

I remember one particular week when we sent a seed-faith offering to a ministry in New Mexico. The woman who is the head of that organization telephoned my office and burst into tears as she asked my secretary, "How did Richard know that today was the day they were going to turn off our lights?" When my secretary related her message to me, I replied quickly, "Tell her that Richard didn't know, but God knew."

Our bankers went ballistic when they heard the news. It was impossible for them to understand. "You owe $56 million," they said. "You can't *give* away 10 percent of your daily income." "You just watch me," I declared. From that moment on, we never backed off our commitment to sow our tithes and offerings to God. It was tough at first. I was repeatedly advised not to tithe, but I had taken my stand on the Word of God.

Satan began to play tricks with my mind. He said, "Richard, you've always thought of yourself as a man of integrity. How can you hold off your creditors while you're giving away 10 percent of your income?" The only way I could do it was that I knew no human mind could match my godly spirit and obedience to the Lord.

The wisdom of man pales in comparison to the wisdom of God. No human mind can pour into you what the Spirit of God can pour into you. You can know so much more with your spirit than you can ever know with your mind alone. Even though we desperately needed every penny to pay our bills, we realized that the money could go so much further if we sowed a portion of it as a seed unto God.

Don't misunderstand what I'm saying here. We remained honorable before our creditors and tried our best to pay them according to the agreements we had worked out with them. But we realized that our only hope of deliverance was in the seeds we sowed to God.

I began to meet with representatives from those companies, and I laid my cards on the table. I refused to make any false promises. Instead, I asked them for favor. I asked them to help us by asking them to accept a plan for repaying what we owed. They knew I needed time, and most of them were willing to give us the time we needed. We began to search for ways to pay them off a little bit at a time.

It was humiliating not being able to pay our bills. We had always maintained an outstanding record with our creditors. The bills were piling higher and higher, and the money to pay them was barely trickling in. The Partners who had stayed with us when the crisis hit were extremely faithful in their giving. It just wasn't enough to pay the bills and service the debt.

ORU Almost Went Down the Tubes

It was "hell on wheels" that first brutal summer as president of ORU. I can recall several specific times when there was absolutely no way for us to meet the payroll. Yet, every time the devil slammed our backs against the wall, we continued planting our seeds as though it was going out of style, and God turned Satan away from the door.

WHEN IT SEEMS ALL HOPE IS GONE

As we sowed our seeds to the Lord, He began to multiply them back to us bountifully. After all, He is the One who said, "Give, and it shall be given to you: good measure, pressed down, shaken together, and running over…" (Luke 6:38). The moment we started tithing again, it seemed as if something broke loose in the spirit realm; and little by little the miracles began.

Not long after we had reinstituted our tithing, I was preaching in a church in California, baring my heart to the congregation concerning the gut-wrenching trials we had been going through. At the close of the service, the Spirit of God began moving through the pastor, and he gave me a very reassuring prophetic word from the Lord. He said that because of our faithfulness in tithing, I was going to be greeted with some thrilling news when I returned home.

It was only a day or two later when I received word from an attorney on the East Coast about a very large donation which had been left to the university by one of our long-standing Partners. Of course, the will would have to go through probate court, which would take time, but I knew that sum of money was coming at that time as a direct result of our tithes and offerings to the Lord.

About sixty days later, a man walked into my office and announced, "The Holy Spirit has told me to give you this check." He handed me a check for $1 million dollars. After he left, I took that check and waved it in the devil's face. I exclaimed, "Satan, can you see that? That's my integrity. That's what the Bible said would come to pass if we would be obedient and tithe." At that instant, the Lord asked me a question which I did not want to hear. He said to me, "Richard, what is the tithe of a $1 million?"

I stammered nervously, "That would be $100,000." You see, tithing was fine with me as long as it involved smaller amounts of money. But now the tithe check had grown to $100,000, and it didn't sound like such a good idea after all. I gulped hard and then hesitantly asked the Lord, "God, do You know how many bills I could pay with $100,000?"

"Richard, what was it that got you that $1 million in the first place?" He replied emphatically.

"Where do You want me to send the checks?" I asked. I started writing out the tithe checks that very afternoon. I knew that no human mind could match my godly spirit and obedience.

Fighting the Demons Within

In spite of all the unbelievable miracles God performed for us, by the time fall rolled around, it looked as though we would have to close the doors of ORU. I had been fighting my heart out, spiritually wrestling demonic powers all summer long. No matter how feverishly we worked, sweated, and prayed, it still looked as though ORU was going down for the count. In my mind I began to draft a letter to the students. We would have to tell them, "Don't come to ORU this fall because we're closing the university. We're padlocking the doors."

There was another critical issue that I was also facing at that time. All of my life I've felt as though I were living in a glass house. Even as a young boy, I was under intense scrutiny. I was constantly being badgered with comments such as, "Oh, you're Oral Roberts' son. How are you ever going to fill his shoes?"

I can remember when I was a boy how I would stuff tissues into the toes of my dad's shoes so I could keep them from flopping off my feet when I tried them on. But his shoes were too big for me. When you're the son of a man who has accomplished something extraordinary in life, you face a hard road. Everybody wonders about you and speculates about whether or not you'll ever be able to fill your father's shoes. A long time ago, I came to grips with the fact that my size $9^1/_2$ foot is never going to fill my dad's size 11 shoes. But I can fill my own shoes. God doesn't expect us to fill anybody else's shoes. He only expects us to be what He created us to be.

The harder I fought to drive the wolves away from ORU's doors, the more I felt as if my knees were buckling under the load. My mind was screaming, *What if I fail?* I believe the fear of failure is perhaps even more paralyzing than failure itself. Why? Fear of failure is like falling asleep with the TV on. When you wake up, it's still droning in the background. The fear of failure is constantly swirling around in your head, mocking and taunting you day and night.

I could read the handwriting on the wall. I knew that Satan had ORU in a deadly stranglehold, and he was determined to snuff it out. I felt as if I had been set up. I began to wish they had never elected me president in the first place. If only my father had remained president for a few more years. Then, if Satan had carried out his death threat against ORU, he could have done it under my dad's tenure and not mine.

I was miserable. I had developed an ulcer. I was angry, bitter, frustrated, and mad at God. I cried out, "Lord, have You raised me up and trained me all of my life just to be embroiled in this mess?" I felt like a rubber band that was stretched taut all the time. Day after day, I was haunted by images of padlocks swinging from the university's doors. I could even picture the sheriff's auction, with the bankers coming in to take over and the creditors swarming like vultures all over our property. In my mind's eye, I could see us conducting the biggest garage sale the world has ever known.

The devil had painted a grim picture for me. I knew I was going to get blamed for ORU going down the tubes.

Operating in Crisis Mode

I'm proud to have a wife who stands beside me as a true Bible wife in every sense of the word—she is my helpmate, the mother of my children, my sweetheart, and my partner in the healing Gospel of Jesus. Lindsay has stood faithfully by my side through the good times as well as the bad. She's been with me every step of the way through this terrible ordeal.

I know she is too dignified to tell you some of the stories she could tell, but I've asked her to share in her own words just how miserable I had become:

After thirteen years of marriage to Richard, the pressure of being president of ORU started shoving him down until it seemed like he was living at the bottom of the barrel. When I looked at my precious husband, all I could see was a $56 million debt wrapped around his neck like a ball and chain. I watched this man, who has never been the type to get overwhelmed by anything, as he began to sink lower and lower. He was caught in the grip of a yoke of bondage.

Every day I saw Richard slipping deeper into a pit of depression. I saw nights when he never slept, days when he just paced the floor. I saw all the times that he didn't spend with his children, and he had always been very attentive to the girls. It seemed as if my Richard were gone and a total stranger had moved into our household in my husband's body. The debt, the bills, the pressure, and the obstacles were consuming his entire life. It was torture watching him suffer, and I felt helpless as he sank lower and lower into the pit.

My practical jokes have always been funny to Richard, but eventually even I couldn't make him laugh. Nothing was funny to him anymore. The huge mountain of problems began to overwhelm him and push him down. My Richard was gone, and I didn't know how to get him back.

My husband had a heavy heart. Proverbs 17:22 (KJV) says, "A broken spirit drieth the bones." I believe Richard's bones were drying up from the inside out. He definitely had a broken spirit. It seemed as if everything about him were broken.

Every morning he went through terrible financial struggles at ORU, and then the rest of the day I would see him walking around like a zombie. Just about the time he thought he had heard the worst possible news, someone would zap him with another piece of news that was even more horrifying. The troubles at ORU were driving him into the ground.

Then one day the devil started talking to my husband, saying, "In less than one year I'm going to destroy what it took your father thirty years to build." At that point in the natural, it appeared that's exactly what was going to happen.

No matter how hard we tried to believe God, we couldn't seem to make even a tiny dent in that gigantic wall of debt. We couldn't chip away at it or see the end of it. We couldn't see a way around it. We couldn't penetrate it. It was like banging our heads against a solid brick wall. We were getting absolutely nowhere.

One day it hit me: Richard is slipping away from us. He's so overwhelmed by this debt that he doesn't notice anything or anyone else. He couldn't see me or the girls. For instance, one night I almost blew myself up. We have a gas grill in our house, and I had turned on the pilot light so I could light the grill, but I didn't realize I had turned the gas up too high. When I lit the torch, I literally blew myself all the way across the room and slammed into the wall.

Thank God, I wasn't killed, but when I reached up and ran my fingers through my hair, a huge hunk of hair came off in my hand. I had blown the top part of my hair off! My eyelashes were gone. My eyebrows were just little tiny black stubs that you could wipe away with your hands. All you could smell was the stench of singed hair.

The girls and I were the only ones at home at the time, and we were so relieved that I hadn't been killed that we burst out laughing. It really was funny how ridiculous I looked with this huge mountain of hair on top of my head and one big bald spot right in the front.

I said to the girls, "I'll bet your dad won't even notice my hair." That's how bad things had gotten in our household. We decided to play a game at the dinner table. "Don't say a word to Dad about Mom's hair and see if he even notices." Do you know that Richard sat through that entire dinner and didn't notice my hair at all? There were little stubs of hair sticking out of my head, and he didn't even see it. Now that's preoccupied.

The girls and I sat there, glancing back and forth at each other across the dinner table, until finally they started chuckling, and I couldn't hold it any longer. "Richard," I asked slowly, "do you notice anything different about me?" My poor husband stared straight at me and said, "No." The girls and I burst into laughter.

"I blew the hair completely off the front of my head!" I exclaimed. "I have no eyelashes, no eyebrows." He looked at me with a blank expression on his face and whispered, "Oh." That was when I knew how desperate things were. I realized then how far we had gone, how deep we had gotten, and how dark it had become in our household. Richard was still our wonderful, precious, loving husband and father, but he was totally preoccupied, eaten alive by this horrible mountain of bills and debt. That's when I told the Lord, "Something has got to change."

When that first disastrous summer drew to a close, I felt as if I had come to the end of the road. From one week to the next, we were barely making the payroll. Many of our creditors were now calling every day.

I would lie awake at night, tossing and turning, with the words Billy Graham spoke at ORU's dedication echoing in my spirit: "If this institution ever moves away from faith in the Bible, and faith in God, and putting God first, then let us this day pronounce a curse on it." I was under a heavy charge from the Lord, and the weight of it was always upon me. I knew ORU was worth giving my life for, but I felt as if I were living on the edge of a hurricane.

It wasn't difficult for me to grasp why a man like King David would cry out, "Oh that I had wings like a dove! I would fly away and be at rest" (Ps. 55:6). I desperately wanted a ticket out. I wanted to hop on an airplane and fly away to the farthest corner of the earth where nobody knew me. Really, I wanted to just bury my head under the covers and never come out, but I had no intention of presiding over the death and burial of the university God had raised up.

Chapter 9

Climbing Out of Hell

Elisha was a man who had the power of God in his life. When one of the sons of the prophets dropped an ax head into the Jordan River, Elisha slashed a branch off a nearby tree and threw it into the water, and the ax head swam to the top! (2 Kings 6:1-6.) The Bible also describes how he threw a bowl of salt into a well of bad water and God healed the water. (2 Kings 2:19-22.)

One of the most unusual miracles of his ministry is found in 2 Kings 4:1-7. One day the wife of one of Elisha's Bible school students went to him with some dreadful news. She told him, "My husband has died, and now his creditor says that he is coming to take my two sons to make them his slaves. Elisha, my sons are all I have left." This story from the Bible is so real. There are people all across this country today who cringe every time the telephone rings because they're afraid it's another creditor threatening to take away their car, their home, their possessions—everything they hold dear.

I know what it feels like to have creditors breathing down my neck, threatening to close the doors of Oral Roberts University. I don't know if you realize how precious this place is to me. If anything bad ever happened to ORU, it would be as if a part of my own life were snuffed out.

We're raising up world-changers, young men and women who are changing the face of this earth for the Gospel. Our students are on fire for the Lord, and they're doing something powerful for the kingdom of God. We're training a generation of young people to be the leaders of tomorrow. They are full of the Word and the Holy Spirit and are going out into every man's world—into the banking industry, government, education, ministry, and many other areas of life—with the good news of the Gospel of Jesus Christ. That's why this widow's story hits home with me. I know what it feels like to have Satan try to snatch something away from you that's irreplaceable.

I want you to notice that when Elisha heard the widow's tragic story, his first response was, "What shall I do for you?" or, "What can I do about it?" Isn't that often our reaction when someone tells us about a terrible financial tragedy? We would love to be able to pay off the person's debts, but more often than not, we can't.

Undoubtedly, Elisha wasn't in a position to pay this woman's bills either, but he wasn't thinking about her problem in the natural. Sometimes I think we miss the whole point when we are naturally minded. We may not be able to pay off another person's debt, but we *can* pray for them. We *can* speak a word of encouragement to lift their spirits. We *can* give them the Word of God. Perhaps we can give them a word of deliverance.

At first Elisha responded in the flesh when he asked, "How can I help you?" Then the power of God began to move on him and he stepped over into the supernatural realm. When you move in the supernatural, you're moving in the realm of miracles. You're stepping into a holy flow of God's presence as you press into the realm of the Spirit. When you enter that realm, you can expect God to give you fresh revelation and a way to escape the devil's attack.

When Elisha began to tune in to the Spirit of God, the Lord prompted him to ask this widow an odd question. "What do you have in your house that you can sell?" he asked. No doubt she must have scratched her head and thought about it for a moment. Then she replied, "The only thing I have is a little jug of oil." A light bulb must have flashed on in Elisha's spirit when she spoke those words.

As soon as he realized that her deliverance depended on God's multiplying her jug of oil, he began to get excited. He knew the only thing that could limit her miracle was the degree to which she pressed in to the Lord with her faith. So he told her, "Borrow as many jars from your friends and neighbors as you possibly can."

I want you to think about this part of the miracle for a moment. What if she had gone to her friends and neighbors and halfheartedly gathered up only a meager supply of jars? She wouldn't have received her miracle. Her miracle depended upon her full obedience to Elisha's instructions. She couldn't have gathered up a few measly jars and expected to receive her full deliverance. It wouldn't have worked. The oil could only be multiplied as long as there were jars to be filled.

What am I driving at here? God asks for our *complete* obedience, not *partial, halfway,* or *halfhearted* obedience. Isaiah 1:19 declares, "If you are willing *and* obedient, you shall eat the good of the land." Being willing speaks of an attitude of the heart. Mere outward obedience to God's Word won't produce much of a breakthrough in your life. When you have a willing heart, spirit, and obedience, the sky is the limit.

Closing the Door on Distractions

The widow gathered up huge armloads of jars—as many as she could find. She and her sons then carefully followed the rest of Elisha's instructions. He told her, "Go into your house with your sons and shut the door behind you. Pour the oil into the jars, and set them aside as they are filled." (2 Kings 4:3,4.)

Why do you suppose Elisha told them to go into their house and shut the door behind them? Most people would shut the door anyway. I believe he didn't want to take any chances, so he spelled out his instructions step by step.

This woman and her sons were desperate. Their hope was almost gone. First, her husband had died, and then his creditors were threatening to tear the rest of the family apart.

There are times in our lives when we have to close the door on everything that would keep us from receiving our miracle. We have to shut the door on the detractors, the critics, and the skeptics. We have to close the door on all the distractions of this life, the cares of this world, and the "busyness" of our daily affairs. When you need a miracle, you had better learn how to shut the door on *anything* that would keep you from pressing in to God.

When the widow shut the door and she and her sons got alone with the Lord, something explosive began to happen in the spirit realm. Her little jug of oil began to bubble and hum and burst with the life of God. Miracle-working power began to flow in her house.

As she called to her sons and told them to start passing her the jars, she must have bowed her head and whispered a prayer. Then perhaps she took a deep breath and began to pour. As she poured, the oil sloshed to the top of those bottles, and as soon as each one was full, she set it aside.

The whole room must have been jammed with jars, all filled to the brim with olive oil. Her sons had probably lined them up across the tabletops and countertops and even piled them all over the floor. What a sight. A few hours earlier as she sat in her house, with tears streaming down her cheeks, not knowing what to do or which way to turn, this widow never dreamed that such a miracle was possible. Her miracle was happening right before her very eyes.

"Bring me another jar!" she exclaimed to her sons, who were just as flabbergasted as she was by the astonishing miracle God was performing for them.

"There aren't any more," they cried, and the Bible says that the oil stopped flowing. The widow went back to Elisha and told him what had happened. He then gave her the rest of the miracle. He said, "Go, sell the oil, and pay your debts; and there will be enough money left over for you and your sons to live on."

The Lord doesn't shut off His miracle power just as soon as our bare, essential needs are met. No, He gives us that extra, "running over" portion. He takes care of our needs, but then He gives us that extra supply to put us over the top. That's what my dear friend, Jesse Duplantis, means when he says, "God is not enough. He's too much."

The apostle Paul put it this way: "Now glory be to God who by his mighty power at work within us is able to do far more than we would ever dare to ask or even dream of—infinitely beyond our highest prayers, desires, thoughts, or hopes" (Eph. 3:20 TLB).

When you're on the brink of despair, do what this widow did. Pour out what you have to the Lord, then watch our "too much" God *pour out* His abundant overflow into your life.

Chapter 10

Obediently Following God

There was a time when we had to have $1.1 million within only a few days or we could kiss the whole thing good-bye. A certain group was planning to file a lien against ORU, and I had convinced them to give me a thirty-day "stay of execution" so I could try to raise the money. Can you imagine what the headlines splattered across the newspapers would look like if somebody slapped a $1.1 million lien on ORU? Can you imagine how that story could get twisted by the TV news?

As we gathered around the conference table for our management meeting that Tuesday, our faces were deathly solemn. We were almost in a state of shock. We knew what was looming before us, but we had no idea where the answer was coming from. A strong word of prophecy came forth that day, commanding us to stand still and see the salvation of the Lord.

When the deadline hit a few days later, we still didn't have the $1.1 million. I had raised a significant portion of it, but not the full amount. I arranged a meeting with a representative of that group, desperately hoping they would accept the money I had raised in lieu of the full amount. However, the man replied, "Cannot do." As he was on his way out the door to go to the courthouse to file the lien, he turned to me and said, "If you can get the rest of the money by 8:30 tomorrow morning, the lien can be removed before anyone sees it."

God Always Comes Through

I was exceedingly grateful for that piece of information, and when I got back to my office, I had an old-time, Holy Ghost prayer meeting with the Lord. I mean, I was praying fervently, earnestly, with tears bursting from my eyes. It looked as though it was all over for Oral Roberts University.

Just a few minutes later, my secretary buzzed me and said that one of our ORU graduates from Oklahoma City was outside waiting to see me. He was a young man whom I had helped get through ORU on a music scholarship, and he had gone on to become a music minister for a church in Oklahoma City. I didn't have a clue as to what he wanted, but I was still happy to see him. I told my secretary, "Sure, send him in."

When that young man walked into my office, he had a peculiar look on his face. "Richard," he said slowly, "I did some work for a man in Oklahoma City, and he asked me to deliver this gift to you for the university." Then he handed me an envelope. When I opened it, my eyes came out on stems. Inside was a check for $1 million to Oral Roberts University.

I laughed, I cried, I jumped, I screamed, and I hollered. I grabbed that guy, and we did a hallelujah dance all around my office, waving that million-dollar check in the air. I rushed right down to deliver the money to our creditor, and at 8:30 the next morning, they removed the lien which had been filed against ORU at 5:00 the previous day.

I don't believe it's any coincidence that this miracle occurred within thirty days after we had reinstituted our tithing.

The Favor of God

My mind goes back to another crisis which erupted during that first horrible summer as president of ORU. A certain bank debt was unexpectedly called in for payment. We were scrambling to pay it, but there was just no way. I rushed downtown to meet with the leadership of that bank, and I poured out my heart to them concerning the harrowing details of what I'd been through that summer.

Much to my astonishment, they told me, "Richard, there was a time when Oral Roberts University stood with our bank when we had a need. Now we're going to stand with you." That bank actually loaned us the money to pay off that debt. I tell you, that's the amazing grace of Jesus Christ in action. In the following months, God blessed us doubly, and we were able to wipe out that entire debt.

Every time another bill was staring us in the face, Satan would rear his ugly head and sneer, "You've made it so far, but you will not make it this time." We'd slip all the way out to the edge—you know what I mean by "the edge," with absolutely no prospect of deliverance. Somehow, God would send another miracle our way.

I have never prayed, "Give us this day our daily bread," in such earnest as I did that first summer as president of ORU. It was like gathering manna from heaven one day at a time. There simply were no leftovers. Thank God, the debt began to take a nosedive. First it dropped to $52 million, then $48 million, then $45 million.

Listening to the Voice of the Spirit

One time I was facing a certain business deal concerning a "depressed" piece of property which the university owned. Have you ever been depressed over a depressed piece of property? The bankers who held the note on that property began to put the squeeze on me, pressuring me to sell it. They informed me that an investment group had offered the appraisal price for it, and they were ecstatic. "You've got to sell it for the $3.3 million," they exclaimed.

I'll admit it was a very tempting offer. As I began to seek the Lord, the Holy Spirit spoke to me and said, "Don't sell that property until you get $5 million for it."

"God, it's not worth $5 million," I shuddered. Yet, He kept impressing me not to accept anything less than $5 million.

The next time the bankers approached me about the deal, I informed them, "There's just one slight problem. The Holy Spirit has told me to hold out for $5 million." I wish you could have seen the look that flashed across one banker's face. At first it was merely a strained look, then a look of utter disbelief. They told me in no uncertain terms, "You should sell that property at the appraised value. It's a good price." But I said no.

Several weeks later the bankers called me one more time and said, "Mr. Roberts, you've won. We've received an offer of $3.8 million for that piece of property. That's half a million dollars more than the appraised value," they said.

I still had one problem. The Holy Spirit had said not to take less than $5 million. This time the bankers were outraged and chewed me out royally. They informed me, "You won't get one penny more for that piece of property." And when I left their office, I felt as if I needed to bandage myself up because of the verbal whipping I had taken. I had decided, however, that I was going to obey God no matter what.

By this time, quite a few people were beginning to think I was crazy, and I was starting to ask the Lord myself, "God, are You sure about this?" But I held on to the amount that I believed He had given me.

It was only a few months later when another group surfaced, and they handed me a check for $5 million for that piece of property. After we had closed the deal, the bankers were flabbergasted. They came to my office and told me sheepishly, "We didn't believe it would happen."

"I know you didn't believe," I replied, "but I did."

"Well, we have to take our hats off to you for making that deal," they continued.

"Don't give me any credit," I insisted. "The Holy Spirit told me not to take anything less than $5 million for that piece of property, and God is the One who gave us the $5 million for it."

When you get a word from the Lord, don't ever let go of it. It may not come to pass immediately, but you're not in charge of the time frame. God has the ultimate time frame. We always try to convince the Lord to go along with our timing, but if we'll stick to His timing, we'll get the results we're looking for. Why? Because no human mind can match our godly spirit and obedience.

The Battle Is the Lord's

Let's look at the story of David and the giant Goliath in 1 Samuel 17 again. I'm captivated by this story because David realized that no human mind could match his godly spirit and obedience to the Lord. This is the story of a great battle—a battle between all the forces of good and the forces of evil, a battle between the expeditionary forces of the Lord and all the demons amassed by Satan himself.

This is a battle between two armies—the army of the Philistines and the army of the living God. It's a battle between the Lord's champion and the devil's champion—a battle between Goliath, a giant nine feet tall, and a young shepherd boy who was almost totally unarmed. This isn't merely a story that took place thousands of years ago. It's so up-to-date that it could have appeared in the newspaper today. This is the kind of battle that is being waged in the lives of people everywhere. It's raging against your life, and it's raging against mine.

Now picture this scene. On one side of the valley was the camp of the Israelites, where King Saul and all of his soldiers were huddled in fear around their campfires. On the other side of that valley was the camp of the Philistines, where the undisputed champion of the day, a giant named Goliath, roared his threats at Israel day and night. For forty days Goliath had strutted back and forth, bellowing out his message, "Send me a man." I mean, he had reduced the fight from a battle between two armies to a fight between two men. "If he defeats me," he yelled, "we'll be your slaves. But if I defeat him, Israel will serve the Philistines." (vv. 8,9.)

When King Saul and his armies heard Goliath's threats, they shivered with fear and their hearts turned to water. Even King Saul himself had lost heart. Everyone was paralyzed with fear. If the devil has another name, it's fear.

Let me take you to another scene miles away on the hillsides of Bethlehem, where a young shepherd boy got a call from his father to take provisions to his older brothers who were serving in the army on the front lines with King Saul.

Standing Up to the Devil

When David arrived at the camp that day, he heard Goliath shouting out his blasphemies at the armies of the living God, and he saw the giant swaggering back and forth across the valley. David whirled around to the men standing nearby. "Is there not a cause?" he cried. (v. 29.) "Isn't there somebody who will take on this godless Philistine?"

His brothers blew a fuse when they heard his words. They were furious at their younger brother, thinking he was trying to show them up. The eldest brother growled at him, "You little pip-squeak. We know all about you. We know you're just trying to get attention!"

When word of David's boldness reached King Saul, he summoned the boy before him and looked him up and down. David volunteered to take on the giant.

"Son," Saul said, "that giant is nine feet tall and armed for battle. How on earth could you hope to take him on and come out alive? Why, have you seen his spear? It's massive. He's been a warrior from his youth, and you're a mere boy."

David reassured Saul, saying, "Sir, when I was tending my father's flocks, one day a lion leaped out of the woods and snatched one of my lambs, and a bear also charged the flock. I yanked that lion to the ground by his beard and slew him, and then I tore the bear limb from limb with my bare hands. The same God who delivered me out of the paws of the lion and the bear will deliver me from this uncircumcised Philistine." (vv. 34-37.)

No doubt King Saul shoved his hands down in his pockets, took a deep breath, and stared straight into David's eyes. After a few moments, he must have shrugged his shoulders and growled, "Well, you don't *look* the part, but you certainly do *sound* the part." Saul added, "David, before you go, put on my armor. Take my sword and my shield—all the weapons I would use if I were going into battle."

Isn't it wonderful that King Saul was willing to give David his full suit of armor, while he went over and hid from the giant in the shadow of the mountain? David refused Saul's offer. In essence, he replied, "O King, this isn't a battle between flesh and blood. This isn't a fight with earthly weapons. This is God's battle. And it's not by might, nor by power, but by God's Spirit that I'll win this fight." (Zech. 4:6.) David realized that no human mind could match his godly spirit and obedience.

The battle that you're embroiled in right now—against sickness, demon power, and Satan's onslaught on your children, your marriage, and your finances—that battle is the Lord's. Yes, you're in the conflict, but it's not your fight. The Lord will fight for you, and He *always* wins His battles.

Goliath Meets His Waterloo

I can see Goliath standing in the middle of the valley, motionless, casting a giant shadow across the hillsides. David knew the pressure was on. The future of Israel was hanging in the balance. The Bible says that he ran to meet Goliath. I can hear him whispering to himself, "Yea, though I walk through the valley of the shadow of death, I will fear no evil; for You are with me; Your rod and Your staff, they comfort me" (Ps. 23:4).

David had his shepherd's stick in one hand and his slingshot in the other. He had practiced with it since he was a boy and knew exactly how to slide that stone into the sling. He knew the proper angle to throw it and the right moment to release it. He also knew that when he released the stone, he had to release his faith to God.

I can see David taunting Goliath and waving his staff at him, drawing the giant's attention away from the slingshot that was tucked away behind his back. I believe David had a firm grasp of military strategy, and he was merely coaxing Goliath to let his defenses down. All at once the giant sneered at him, "What am I, a dog that you come at me with a stick?" He cursed David and added, "Come on up here, boy, and I'll feed your flesh to the birds of the air and the wild animals." (1 Sam. 17:43,44.)

David shouted back at him, "You come to me with your sword and your spear and your shield, but I come against you in the name of the Lord of hosts—the God you've defied. And this day He will deliver you into my hands." (vv. 45,46.)

I can imagine Goliath's shield-bearer stumbling to his knees, howling with laughter when he heard those words. I can hear Goliath starting to chuckle, his huge body shaking as he throws his head back and begins to roar with laughter.

Goliath laughed so hard that he must have had to raise the visor on his headgear to get a better look at the little pip-squeak who was darting toward him, waving a stick in the air. But as soon as he lifted his visor, his forehead was exposed. There was only one vulnerable spot on the giant's body, and when he shoved his visor back to see that puny little teenager who was huffing and puffing up the hillside, he exposed that vulnerable spot for everybody to see. You'd better watch out, Goliath. You're about to meet your Waterloo.

And Satan had better watch out in your life, too, because God is about to slam the door shut on the devil's agenda.

While Goliath was standing with his defenses down, jeering at the young shepherd boy who was coming at him with a stick, David was busy loading his slingshot behind his back. He had his eyes fastened on the exposed spot on Goliath's forehead, and he began to swing that slingshot around and around his head. Like a bolt of lightning, David's stone catapulted from its socket. As it whizzed through the air, no doubt he was saying, "Lord, as I release this stone, I'm releasing my faith to You."

That stone went hurtling through the air, and it struck Goliath in the forehead. The giant sank to the ground. The force of the blow merely dazed him, so David took Goliath's own sword—a big, long blade—and killed him with it and cut off his head. (vv. 49-51.)

In the sweep of a moment, the armies of Israel began to cheer wildly as they chased the Philistines across that valley, cutting off their heads and strewing their bodies on the ground for the fowls of the air to devour. Israel's enemies became their slaves because David realized that no human mind could match his godly spirit and obedience to the Lord.

God Will Fight for You

The story of David and Goliath is more than just a mere story. It's your story and my story. It's your faith and my faith talking. It's you and me standing up with every fiber of our being and proclaiming, "The battle is the Lord's. And in the name of Jesus Christ of Nazareth, I will not allow any situation to steal my hope. I will walk through the valley of the shadow of death and cut off the giant's head. I refuse to put up with this satanic attack any longer."

It looked absolutely ridiculous for David to take on that towering giant, armed with only a slingshot and his shepherd's staff. It looks just as ridiculous for you or me to try to take on a great big giant of a problem, armed with only our Bibles and our faith.

Remember, no human mind can match your godly spirit and obedience, and the Lord of the universe is the One who fights for you. It's not by might nor by power that you can win your battle. It's the Spirit of the Lord who puts the enemy to flight.

Chapter 11

Giving the Devil the Boot

Have you ever felt as if Satan were shooting his biggest guns at you and you couldn't find any place to hide? Or have you watched in horror as everybody around you seemed to collapse under his deadly barrage?

Isaiah 36 tells the story of a king of Israel named Hezekiah who must have felt exactly that way. King Sennacherib of Assyria had already plundered the other great cities of Judah. He sent his messenger with a large army to Jerusalem to try to bully King Hezekiah into surrendering to him.

Just think about this scene for a moment. All the other cities in Judah had already fallen to the Assyrians. Why should Jerusalem be any different? Isn't that the way the devil comes against your life? Doesn't he tell you, "Everybody else's life is coming apart; what makes you think your life is going to be any different?"

Don't listen to the devil's threats. In Psalm 91:7 the Lord said, "A thousand may fall at your side, and ten thousand at your right hand; but it shall not come near you." Isaiah 54:17 also declares, "No weapon formed against you shall prosper...." Take your stand on God's Word and expect Him to deliver you.

King Hezekiah sent his men out to meet with Sennacherib's messenger, and the man immediately began to rail at them. First he snarled, "Why don't you ask Hezekiah who he's trusting in?" He continued, "If you really think you're trusting in the Lord, then let me ask you one question. Why should God do anything for you since Hezekiah is the one who knocked down all of His high places and altars and commanded the people to go to Jerusalem and worship the Lord?"

The Devil's Lies

The devil loves to come at you with a bunch of half-truths. Yes, Hezekiah *did* knock down the high places and altars throughout the land of Israel, but they were places of idol worship, not places where the people worshiped God.

In Isaiah 36:8-9 Sennacherib offered King Hezekiah a wager. He said, "If you can produce two thousand men in your army, I'll give you two thousand horses for them to ride." Then the messenger sneered, "With that tiny little army of yours, how can you possibly think about attacking even the smallest and worst contingent of my well-trained troops?"

It was true that Hezekiah's armies were no match for the massive armies of Assyria. And it's true that in the natural, you're no match for the devil's assault against your life. The odds may be stacked against you. You may have received a shocking diagnosis of some incurable disease in your body. It may look as if your world has toppled upside down. Satan may have a million-to-one odds against you, but our God can change the odds so fast that it will make the devil's head spin.

I want you to notice Satan's next strategy. In Isaiah 36:10 the Assyrian messenger declared, "The Lord has sent me to destroy your land." All of a sudden the devil himself is claiming to be on a mission for God.

As soon as the messenger uttered those words, Hezekiah's men exclaimed, "Why don't you speak in the Syrian language, since we understand it well? Don't speak in Hebrew because the people on the wall will hear you." That just egged him on more. He began to shout in Hebrew, "My master wants everyone in Jerusalem to know that if you don't surrender, this city will be besieged by the armies of Syria until everyone is so hungry and thirsty that he will eat his own dung and drink his own urine." (v. 12.)

The devil is a bully, and he loves to shout his tirades. First Peter 5:8 says that he goes about *like* a roaring lion. He is *not* a lion. The only teeth he has are the teeth you give him when you believe in his threats *more* than you believe in the promises of God.

In Isaiah 36:14 the messenger shouted to the people of Jerusalem, "Don't let Hezekiah try to tell you that the Lord will deliver you. Have any of the gods of other nations delivered them from the king of Assyria?" He then tried to make a deal with them.

The devil is always ready to try to make a deal with you. He'll say, "If you'll just go along with this one issue, just bend a little here, be flexible there, it will go well with you." Pretty soon he'll strap a yoke of compromise around your neck, and you'll be wondering how on earth you got mixed up in that particular situation.

The messenger told the people, "The king of Assyria says, 'If you'll surrender to me, I'll let each one of you have your own farm and garden and water. I'll make arrangements to take you to a land very much like your own—a land of corn and wine, a land of bread and vineyards.'" The devil promises you everything, but he delivers nothing except pain and heartache and destruction and doom.

I want you to notice how the people of Jerusalem responded to the threats of the Assyrians. Verse 21 says, "They held their peace and answered him not a word; for the king's commandment was, 'Do not answer him.'" They didn't try to carry on a conversation with the devil. Don't you get into a conversation with him either. Don't try to argue with Satan. Instead, begin to quote the Word of God and watch him flee.

God's Got Your Back

In chapter 37 Hezekiah's men reported to him what the messenger had said, and he tore his clothes and covered himself with sackcloth as a sign of humility and mourning. Then he went into the temple to pray. Hezekiah knew that his only hope was in the Lord.

At the same time, he sent his prime minister and the older priests with a message for the prophet Isaiah. In other words, not only did he seek the Lord in prayer, but he also linked up his faith with a man of God. He told Isaiah, "This is a day of terrible trouble and distress, but perhaps the Lord has heard how the king of Assyria has scoffed at *Him.* Surely God won't let him get away with it." (vv. 3,4.)

Always remember that when Satan comes against your life, he isn't attacking just you. You're God's child, and that means he's also attacking God and His Word. When the devil tries to twist the Word of God, you have every right to say, "Lord, Satan is trying to make You look bad, but I don't believe You're going to let him get away with it." That's what Hezekiah was saying.

After Isaiah had received the king's prayer request, he sent this message back to him: "The Lord says, 'Do not be afraid of what you've heard from the servants of the king of Assyria. He's going to hear a rumor of trouble in his own land, and he will return home. I will cause him to die by the sword there.'" (vv. 6,7.) When your hope seems gone, isn't it wonderful to get a word from the Lord in the middle of adversity?

Isaiah 37:9 says that Sennacherib received a report that the king of Egypt was marching out to attack him, so he quickly made plans to return home. Before he left, he dispatched a letter to King Hezekiah, which was filled with more death threats. The letter read, "Hezekiah, don't let your God deceive you when He says that Jerusalem will not be handed over to the king of Assyria." (v. 10.) Isn't that exactly how the devil talks to you when you receive a word from the Lord? Doesn't he challenge what you believe you've heard from your heavenly Father? That's the way Satan talked to King Hezekiah.

The king of Assyria questioned him, "What makes you think your God will be able to deliver you when none of the gods of the other nations have been able to keep them from falling into my hands?" He then began to name a long list of all the other kings he had already crushed.

Satan still sings the same old song to you and me today. Let's suppose for a moment that you've received a diagnosis of cancer in your body. The first thing Satan does is tell you that you're going to die. His next strategy is to bombard your mind with thoughts of other people who have died from cancer—especially good, Christian people. Next he taunts you with the words, "What makes you think you're going to be any different?"

Listen to what God has to say about that. Second Corinthians 10:12 says that we should *not* compare ourselves with others. Only God knows what happened in those cases where someone died an untimely death. The bottom line is this. Even if a terrible plague sweeps the entire globe, if you believe God's Word concerning healing, you can be the only person on earth who survives that plague. Your fate ultimately depends on your believing God and His Word.

Trust in God No Matter What

You may say, "But, Richard, my father and mother both died of cancer." Their fate does not determine your fate. I realize that heredity plays a part in every person's health, but you have a choice. You can put your faith in what your heredity says about you, or you can put your faith in what God's Word says about you.

What does God's Word say about your health? Isaiah 53:5 declares, "...by His [Jesus'] stripes we are healed." Matthew 8:17 says,

"...Himself [Jesus] took our infirmities and bore our sicknesses." Third John 2 proclaims, "Beloved, I wish that you may prosper in all things and be in health, just as your soul prospers."

Your heredity may indicate that you are a high risk to have a heart attack, cancer, diabetes, or some other devastating disease, and that is reality. I'm not talking about denying reality. Hezekiah didn't deny the reality that all of the surrounding cities and nations had fallen to Sennacherib's armies. However, he knew that God had a way of turning the devil's reality into a mighty victory for God's people.

As soon as Hezekiah read Sennacherib's letter, he went straight to the temple and laid the letter upon the altar before God. He lifted his voice in praise, worship, and adoration to the Lord and said, "O Lord, You alone are God of all the kingdoms of the earth. You made heaven and earth." Then he continued, "Lord, this arrogant Assyrian king has been mocking You. He's been saying that You can't deliver Your people out of his hand.

"God, it's true that he's already conquered all the surrounding nations and overthrown their gods. They weren't real gods anyway. They were gods made of wood and stone, fashioned by human hands." Then he pleaded with the Lord, "Now, O Lord our God, deliver us from his hand so that all the kingdoms of the earth may know that You alone are God."

God didn't waste one second in answering Hezekiah's prayer. Isaiah sent him a message that was red hot from the Lord, and it contained a strong word for King Sennacherib. He said, "Sennacherib, you have raised your voice against the Holy One of Israel. You have heaped insults upon the Lord. But because you rage against Me, I will put My hook in your nose and My bit in your mouth, and I will make you return by the way you came." (v. 29.) That's exactly what the Lord is telling Satan on your behalf right now. He's telling the devil, "You're going to have to return by the way you came."

God told Hezekiah, "Here is the proof that I am the one who is delivering this city from the king of Assyria: This year he will abandon his siege. Although it is too late now to plant your crops, and you will have only volunteer grain this fall, still it will give you enough seed for a small harvest next year, and two years from now you will be living in luxury again" (Isa. 37:30 TLB).

God doesn't merely want to deliver us out of Satan's clutches. He wants to completely restore what the devil has stolen. He wants us to live in His abundance again.

Don't Mess With God

At the close of these powerful chapters from the book of Isaiah, God gives some of the strongest words the Bible records against an enemy of His people: "He [King Sennacherib] shall not come into this city, nor shoot an arrow there, nor come before it with shield, nor build a siege mound against it. By the way that he came, by the same shall he return; and he shall not come into this city...for I will defend this city, to save it for My own sake..." (vv. 33-35).

The Lord doesn't mess around with the devil when the devil messes around with you. He tells Satan, "I will defend them for My sake and for the sake of My Word." I want you to read what God did to those Assyrian forces: "Then the angel of the Lord went out, and killed in the camp of the Assyrians one hundred and eighty-five thousand; and when people arose early in the next morning, there was corpses—all dead" (v. 36).

No doubt Sennacherib got the message. The Bible says that he immediately broke camp and fled to Nineveh and stayed there. One day as he was worshiping Nisroch, his demon god, two of his own sons stabbed him to death right there in the house of his god. He died in his own land, just as the Lord had predicted. (v. 38.)

This isn't some kind of fairy tale. This is the story of your life and mine, if we'll do what Hezekiah did when our hope seems to be gone. When we call upon the Lord in faith, when we lay Satan's threats upon the altar before God, we can expect Him to make the devil eat his words.

Chapter 12

Is This It?

There was a time in my life when my hope was just about gone. I praise God that He turned my situation around and gave me hope for the future. Even though, in the natural, my situation didn't look much different, I viewed the circumstances through God's eyes, and that made all the difference in the world.

Let me give you a word of warning before you read any further. The following pages are a testimony of how my life went from a hopeless situation that consumed my every thought to a happy, hilarious trust in God. Now, what you're about to read may produce a spontaneous-combustion, Holy Ghost-filled outpouring of joy and laughter that cannot be contained. You may not be able to drive a car for a while after reading this chapter and may need to appoint a designated driver. It might not be a good idea to venture out in public too soon after reading this book. You might also want to warn your family about the hilariously joyful side effects.

Every place I've shared this testimony, there's been a tremendous uncontainable outbreak of holy joy and laughter like I've never seen before. Why don't you let me set the stage for you, and then you'll understand exactly what I'm talking about.

During that first grueling summer as president of ORU, I received an invitation from Pastor Karl Strader, a member of our ORU Board of Regents, to preach at Carpenter's Home Church in Lakeland, Florida.

When I received that invitation, I had absolutely no idea what God had in store for me.

I was so numb from the financial beating I was taking that I felt as if I were crawling around on my belly. I was almost oblivious to the world around me. Like so many Christians today, I was down in my spirit and hurting inside.

Before I boarded the plane for Lakeland, Lindsay said to me, "Richard, something is going to happen to you while you're in Lakeland. You're going to turn a corner in your life and ministry." I mumbled some kind of vague, halfhearted reply. Really, I didn't even have a glimmer of what she was talking about, and secondly, I didn't want to go.

A Mighty Move of God

Above all, I just wasn't impressed. I had heard the stories about the revival of joy that had broken out in Brother Strader's church. I had heard about a young South African evangelist named Rodney Howard-Browne who had preached there and how the Spirit of God had swept over the crowds with indescribable joy and holy laughter.

According to the reports I had heard, this man's ministry was very much like Brother Kenneth Hagin's ministry was when he was in his thirties, with a similar style and moving of the Spirit. Brother Rodney's ministry was built solidly on the Word of God, especially the Scripture in Nehemiah 8:10 which says, "...the joy of the Lord is your strength."

Before this evangelist had conducted a revival for Pastor Strader, Carpenter's Home Church had been ripped apart by a devastating church split, and they had also become strapped with overwhelming financial burdens. In fact, the Straders had almost lost the church.

When Brother Rodney visited the Lakeland area, some five hundred churches cooperated in sponsoring the revival. Almost overnight, Carpenter's Home Church was jammed to the rafters with six to eight thousand people packing the auditorium at ten o'clock on Tuesday, Wednesday, and Thursday mornings. There were overflow crowds of nine to ten thousand every night, six nights a week for eight weeks.

I had heard Pastor Strader describe in vivid detail how he would find himself sprawled on the floor of the church night after night, laughing hysterically in the Spirit. God began to pour out a fresh baptism of holy joy and laughter on the entire Lakeland area.

At one point during that unprecedented revival, they set up a portable swimming pool beside the altar, and some two thousand people were baptized in it. It was the most earthshaking, heaven-moving outpouring of God ever seen in the city of Lakeland.

There's one particular story that stands out in my mind from those amazing Holy Ghost services. One night there was a woman in the congregation who had to work the late shift on her job that night. She slipped out of the auditorium, climbed into her car, and set out on her drive to work. She made a terrible mistake. Halfway there, she turned on the radio and tuned in to the station which was broadcasting the revival. As soon as she heard that Holy Ghost laughter streaming across the airwaves, she became so drunk in the Spirit that she started weaving all over the highway.

A motorcycle officer with the Florida Highway Patrol spotted her and pulled her over. That poor, unsuspecting man walked up to the door of her car and started to write out a ticket. By then she was absolutely shrieking with laughter, and the radio was still blaring. "What are you listening to?" the officer asked her with a puzzled look on his face. Suddenly, she became as sober as a church mouse and started telling him all about the revival, and he was all ears.

In a moment, the officer fell to the ground, laughing uncontrollably in the Spirit. The woman got out of her car and helped him to his feet. When he could finally contain himself, he told her, "I've been running from God for fifteen years." She then led him to Jesus right there beside her car.

The Joy of the Lord

I knew from all the reports I was hearing that this revival of Holy Ghost joy was real. I knew it was a sovereign move of God's Spirit, but I just wasn't interested. Really, it wasn't on my agenda. After all, I had the weight of the whole ORU debt resting on me. I was in no frame of mind to laugh.

I had grown up in certain circles where people did unusual things according to the world's standards. They marched up and down the aisles of the church in a Jericho victory march before the Lord. They sang and shouted and clapped their hands and made a joyful noise unto God, shaking the rafters with the sound of their praise.

I wasn't opposed in any way to what was happening in Pastor Strader's church, but I was the type of person who likes to be in control. I planned to go to Lakeland as scheduled, and I would have my time of ministry there. I then planned to board a flight for Tulsa and fly back home, and that would be that.

I wasn't the least bit startled when Pastor Strader warned me, "Richard, no one has been able to do very much preaching in our church since this revival broke out. Everyone who has visited here has been overtaken by Holy Ghost joy and laughter." He went on to describe a minister whom I've known for more than 20 years who had tried to preach there a few weeks earlier. According to Pastor Strader, when that man stepped onto the platform, his legs immediately buckled beneath him, sending him sprawling onto the floor. He then laid there for a solid hour, convulsing with hysterical laughter.

I knew it wasn't like this particular individual to act that way, but I was so numb from the problems I was grappling with that I mumbled,

"Well, okay, so what?" I couldn't picture myself falling on the floor laughing. Happy, hilarious laughter was the furthest thing in the world from my mind.

When the joy of the Lord came into my life, it came upon me suddenly. I didn't have the faintest idea that God was about to send His holy joy and laughter raining down on me from heaven. If you want to know the real truth of the matter, I was totally put out and disgusted with life.

When I stepped onto the platform at Carpenter's Home Church, I started singing and then immediately launched into my sermon, which I titled, "How To Get Out of Your Present Mess." Really, my message was based upon my own agonizing struggle to break free from the financial mess at ORU.

Miraculous Breakthrough

I was preaching my heart out when, all at once, the Lord gave me a word of knowledge about someone's ear being healed. I called a man out of the crowd, and then God impressed me to lay my hands on him. The instant I touched that man, he started falling to the floor under the power of God. The realization flashed through my mind that no one was there to catch him.

I was holding a microphone in one hand, so I reached around behind him with my other hand to try to catch him. He was a big man, and the force of his fall sent me sailing through the air right over the top of his head. I turned a full somersault over that man's body and landed on my feet on the other side. It was a Holy Ghost somersault. I looked like one of those gymnasts in the Olympics. And, believe me, it was funny. The congregation roared with laughter.

About ten minutes later, they were still laughing, and, to me, it wasn't funny anymore. I looked around that auditorium in amazement as great waves of laughter swept over the crowd. I could see big tears rolling down people's faces, and some people were even falling onto the floor, laughing uncontrollably. Everywhere I looked, all I could see were "holy rollers."

Pastor Strader was laughing so hard that his face was literally streaked with tears. His son Steven, who is an ORU graduate, was down on his hands and knees, pounding the floor with his fists, laughing hysterically. It looked like everyone in the whole church was laughing.

After a few minutes, I glanced over at the pastor and asked him sheepishly, "What is this?"

He said, "This is that."

I said, "What's that?"

He said, "This."

Remember, I had been almost completely without any type of joy or laughter for so many months because of the trials I was going through. When I started laughing that day, it was because that Holy Ghost somersault *was* funny.

All of a sudden, I began to feel the strangest sensation welling up in my belly. It was like a rumbling sensation. I felt something very peculiar bubbling up inside me. It was the same kind of feeling I have when I pray in tongues, but this time I felt laughter flowing up out of my innermost being. I began to laugh when there was no earthly reason to laugh. It wasn't a chest laugh, or a surface laugh, but rather it was laughter that was rolling up from way down deep in my soul. It was joy. It was holy. It was holy laughter. And it could not be contained.

The Scripture in John 7:38 KJV came flooding up in my spirit. It's the passage where Jesus declared, "Out of [your] belly shall flow rivers of living water." The Gospel writer goes on to say that He was speaking of the Holy Ghost, which had not yet been given because Jesus had not yet been glorified.

When the joy of the Lord hit my life, it hit me like a bolt of lightning, and I began to laugh from my belly area in much the same way that I pray in tongues from my belly area. Up until that point, about the only spark of relief I could get from all the hair-raising struggles in my life was by praying in tongues. This holy joy and laughter was giving me a relief from my heartaches like I'd never known before.

I forgot the rest of my sermon and collapsed on the front row of the church, doubled over with Holy Ghost laughter. I was so far gone that I just laid my head down on the lap of the lady next to me, laughing in the Spirit with reckless abandon. The joy of the Lord got all over me more than anyone else, and I needed it desperately. The more I laughed, the more I felt my burdens being stripped away. I felt the fear evaporate, the pressure lighten, and the terrible, mind-boggling stress take wing and fly away.

There was a total rejuvenation of my spirit, soul, and body. I felt as if my entire being had been infused with divine energy from heaven. My troubles hadn't changed one bit, but something inside me was beginning to change.

On the Floor With Holy Ghost Laughter

Later that day, I was burning up the phone lines back to Tulsa, trying to explain to my wife, Lindsay, the astonishing things that had happened to me. "I knew it!" she exclaimed as she rejoiced with me over the telephone. "I knew you were going to turn a corner in your life." Then she added, "Bring it back home to Tulsa. Bring it back to ORU."

For the rest of the afternoon, Pastor Strader tried to explain to me what this baptism of joy was all about, but I still couldn't grasp it. When we arrived at the service that night, the instant he introduced me, I slid right out of my chair onto the floor, and I couldn't get up. I was laughing hysterically in the Spirit.

I felt like such a fool. I mean, you go to church and just fall out of your chair laughing? For about ten minutes I was sprawled out on the floor, laughing uncontrollably, and nothing whatsoever was funny. Brother Strader was trying to carry on the service, while I was lying in a heap on the front row of the church, howling with laughter. I tried to move, but I couldn't budge. It was as if I were nailed to the floor. My body felt as if it weighed a thousand pounds.

Anyone who knows me very well knows that I'm not the type of person who collapses on the floor, rolls around, and convulses with laughter. I'm much too respectable, too dignified, for that. My wife says that I'm very detailed, very methodical. Really, she says that sometimes I'm almost stuffy. I go to bed at night with my pajamas creased, and they're still creased in the morning when I crawl out of bed.

The service was on the radio live that night, so Brother Strader announced, "For the benefit of the radio audience, our evangelist is on the floor." Then he had to kill some time until I could regain my composure. For the next few minutes, he described in vivid detail how God had poured out a fresh baptism of joy in his life during Brother Rodney Howard-Browne's revival. "I kind of had a permanent spot right down there on the floor where I seemed to wind up every night." He exclaimed laughingly, "One night my ushers traced a human outline on that spot, and they wrote on it, *Reserved for Pastor.*"

After Brother Strader had covered for me for at least ten minutes, I finally managed to struggle to my feet. The instant I hit the platform, somebody yelled, "Sing!"

"You've got to be kidding," I gasped. "I can't sing." But I had them go ahead and roll the soundtrack. I got out only about two or three bars of the song before I slumped down onto the platform, shaking with laughter all over again. By that time, the entire congregation was roaring. One man was down on the floor in the aisle on his stomach, laughing and wildly flapping his arms in the air. All I had to do was take one look at him, and I was gone. I must have laughed nonstop for thirty more minutes.

As waves of Holy Ghost laughter rippled across that auditorium, the gifts of the Spirit began to flow. One young woman who had suffered for eight years from a horrible ringing or roaring sound in her ears was perfectly healed by the Lord. I never even touched her. All I did was spit on her—not intentionally, of course. When she came up to give her testimony, I got tickled and burst out laughing in the Spirit, and I accidentally showered her with spit.

What happened to me that weekend in Lakeland, Florida, was nothing short of a sovereign move of God. Once I yielded to the Lord, I became so immersed in His presence that I began to cast myself aside, saying, "Lord, if this is of You, then I must decrease and You must increase. God, I'm putting my life into Your hands."

A very soul-stirring word of prophecy came forth that night from a man in the audience. He said to me, *Richard, I got very emotional when I heard you say you wanted God to give you a fresh anointing. And I'm here to tell you that He has given you that fresh anointing—an anointing of joy—to take back with you to bless your ministry, to bless you as president of that university.*

I am so in awe of the fact that your dad was a stammering, stuttering person who stood in the middle of an empty field and God placed that [calling] on him. And now the mantle is being handed down, and it's going to be a different kind of anointing. It's going to be an anointing of joy and prosperity on that campus like never before.

Brother, I am telling you, you are a different person. God is changing you. Your countenance, your demeanor, is different. People look to you to be this awesome leader, but here you are strewn out on the floor [under the power of the Lord], and I'm impressed with that...because you're willing to submit to the move of the Holy Spirit. That's what He's looking for—a willingness to let go and let God be God.

A New Man

When I boarded my flight for Tulsa the next morning, I had a copy of a new best-seller that I wanted to read. I was sitting there, minding my own business, completely engrossed in this gripping novel when, out of the blue, I burst into sidesplitting laughter right there on the plane.

The person next to me was so startled that he glanced over in my direction, wide-eyed, and started peeking over at the cover of my book to see what on earth I was reading. *When it finally dawned on him that I was reading a high-powered action thriller, he looked at me as if to say, Who is this nut sitting next to me?*

It was only a few moments later when the flight attendant leaned over and whispered, "Is anything wrong?"

"No," I told her between gasps of laughter, and I just kept right on laughing. There I was, reading a spine-tingling book, and I was absolutely roaring. Of course, by then, the man next to me was certain that it was time to send for the straitjacket.

In fact, all the people in my entire section of the plane kept staring at me, but I couldn't have cared less. By the time I had laughed for about ten minutes straight, some of those passengers couldn't control themselves any longer, and they were laughing with me. Why? Laughter is contagious.

When I landed in Tulsa, I could hardly wait for Lindsay to watch the video of those incredible services at Carpenter's Home Church. I wanted her to see her dignified husband rolling around on the floor, laughing hysterically in the Spirit. I've asked her to describe in her own words her reaction the very first time we watched that exciting video:

Richard had tried to explain to me over the telephone what had happened to him in Lakeland, but there was just no way. Finally, he said, "I'm going to bring it home on video." That first night, we stayed up all night and watched that two-hour video three times. That amounts to six hours of laughing in the Spirit.

I'll tell you what—a merry heart did good like a medicine for us that night. We took our Holy Ghost medicine, and we were happy campers even though we had no reason in the natural to be happy.

When I watched the joy of the Lord hit my Richard, I saw Mr. Perfect turn a somersault in mid-air and roll head over heels on the floor of the church. Here's a man who is usually in control. But I watched Mr. Perfect totally lose control. It was the most glorious thing I'd ever seen.

I remember watching that precious young lady who was telling him a tragic story about a very serious hearing problem she had experienced. Right in the middle of what she was saying, the joy hit Richard, and it hit her, and he was laughing so hard that he actually spit in her face. That is not like my husband. That woman, however, had been miraculously healed by the power of God.

All of these years I've seen Richard walk, speak, and live by faith. He's a person who has been completely stable in every area of his life. He doesn't ordinarily have high highs or low lows. Because of the troubles we were facing at ORU, every time we were struck by another problem, I would see it overwhelm and consume him.

After the joy of the Lord came into his life, his entire personality changed. Now, when a problem comes, he isn't consumed by it. Instead, he is consumed by the answer, which is Jesus Christ. He is consumed with the joy of the Lord. No matter what comes at him from the right or the left, from the North, South, East, or West, he handles it by faith and Holy Ghost joy. Really, he has become a new man because of it.

When the joy hit Richard's life, ORU's troubles didn't change overnight. What changed was Richard's inner man. It was the first time I had seen him have a deep inner peace and an overflowing joy in the middle of some of the most horrible, depressing trials that we had ever gone through.

I'm not talking about an emotional outburst—ha-ha-ha, tee-hee-hee—and when the next problem hits, you're dying on the inside. No, God is allowing

Richard to see the problems in a different light, and that has made a big change in him.

Isn't it amazing how you can get down to the rock bottom of life and wonder, Does God even know where I am? He knows. He knew that Richard wasn't going to make it without the joy of the Lord to strengthen him and lift his spirit.

We've always had a happy home and a happy marriage, but today our home is a joy-filled, hilariously happy home. The laughter at our house is contagious, and a merry heart has kept us through all the fiery trials and ordeals that we've faced.

If you've been skeptical about the joy of the Lord, if you think it's some kind of hocus-pocus, all I can tell you is that I saw the joy of the Lord hit my husband—hit his mind, heart, but more than anything else, his spirit. When it hit his spirit, he came home to me a new man. I have my Richard back. I saw my husband completely, 100 percent restored by the joy of the Lord.

Keep Your "Worrier" on the Back Burner

This wasn't some kind of crazy, slapstick comedy adventure that I experienced on my trip to Lakeland, Florida. While I was laughing, chains were being broken in the spirit realm. I felt the load lighten. I felt the dark clouds lift. I felt as if I could fly. All of those awful burdens suddenly began to roll away. I'm not saying those things weren't important anymore, but they no longer had a vise-like grip on me. It was as if God had put all of my worrying on the back burner. You may need God to help you put your worrier on the back burner, too.

When that mighty torrent of Holy Ghost joy came rushing through my life, I had to have it. It was as if I had been out on the windblown sands of the desert for days, under the hot, boiling sun. I don't believe I could have staggered one more step through that barren wasteland if God hadn't come down and lifted the load.

When this joy-filled worship began rolling out of my spirit, I began to change. The stress began to melt away, and the ulcer I had developed was healed. Now I have a *knowing* in my heart, not a *gnawing* in the pit of my stomach. There's a brand-new freedom in my soul that I've never had before. The more I laugh, the more I get into the rhythm of God's Holy Ghost blessings. The Lord is revolutionizing my life through this mighty baptism of joy.

A Holy Ghost Revival of Joy

Can you imagine the thoughts that raced through my mind when I arrived in Tulsa from Lakeland and heard that Rodney Howard-Browne was going to conduct a revival at Rhema Bible Church, just a few miles from the Oral Roberts University campus?

By that time, I wanted to invite Brother Rodney to minister at ORU. I wanted our students, faculty, and staff to experience the same spontaneous, uncontrollable tidal wave of joy and laughter as I had. My parents and Lindsay and I decided to attend several of the services.

It took Lindsay some time to absorb all that was happening. She knew it was real; still, it took awhile for her. But the night came when something sovereign began happening to her too, and we laughed and laughed and laughed. In fact, that night we spent a whole lot of time on the floor, laughing.

I remember one particular service when she fell out of our pew, sprawled on the floor, and ended up directly underneath Brother and Sister Hagin's pew as the joy of the Lord flooded her life.

Another night, Brother Rodney called me up to the platform to give a testimony, and I began by saying, "Well, we've had a $56 million debt," but those were the only words I managed to blurt out. The next thing I knew, I had collapsed on the floor, laughing so hard that it felt as if my sides would split open. While I was lying there, I heard the Holy Spirit speaking in my spirit, *In the same way that you're laughing here tonight,* *you're going to laugh while I pay off your $56 million debt.* Those words meant *everything* to me.

By the time I managed to wobble back to my seat, Lindsay had draped herself across the pew, laughing. "What's all that?" I asked when I saw a huge puddle of spit. "I spit all over the pew," she said, and then she burst out laughing all over again. If I'd had any doubts about whether the joy was real, that put an end to it right there. That's just not Lindsay's style. My wife is really respectable. She's a very dignified lady.

Speaking of dignified ladies, I'll never forget the night my mother, Evelyn Roberts, and Brother Hagin's wife, Oretha, were laughing so hard in the Spirit that they were stumbling and falling down, absolutely drunk in the Holy Ghost. Those are two of the most refined, most lady-like women of God I have ever met. They were having such a hallelujah time that night that they were falling on top of each other, creating a hilarious traffic jam in the hallway of Rhema Bible Church.

As they staggered out of the building that night, they looked like two drunken ladies trying to make their way home after an all-night drinking spree. I knew they hadn't been drinking alcohol. They had been drinking from those rivers of living water that Jesus talked about in John 7:38. They were bursting with Holy Ghost laughter and joy.

My mother told me later, "Richard, when I was a young girl, we were in Pentecostal services where the power of God was so strong that many could not walk home when the service was over. Many just fell onto the floor laughing, and some had to be carried home in carts."

That's when it dawned on me that there had to be a reason why Peter stood up on the Day of Pentecost and announced to the crowd, "These men aren't drunk on alcohol as you suppose they are." (Acts 2:15.) What on earth do you suppose they were doing? Could they have been stumbling down the street, hilariously drunk in the Spirit? Whatever it was, it must have been something that made them appear to be drunk on alcohol. But instead of being drunk on alcohol they were drunk on the new wine of the Spirit.

That fall I invited Brother Rodney Howard-Browne for a Holy Ghost revival at Oral Roberts University, and I shut down the entire campus for two whole days. I wanted all of our faculty, staff, and students to experience an earthshaking, heaven-moving encounter with God.

When he arrived on campus, he began preaching like a man from another world. He poured out Scripture after Scripture on the subject of Bible joy. The atmosphere was electrified as he preached about the outpouring of the Spirit on the Day of Pentecost. He said that God had shown him that the church has lost its joy. Somehow the body of Christ has forgotten that the joy of the Lord is their strength.

He described in vivid detail the mighty revivals from the Day of Pentecost through the present day. We were literally spellbound, sitting on the edges of our seats, as he told about the early revivals which swept like wildfire across the American frontier.

He gave thrilling accounts of the Kentucky outpouring of June 1800, when it was reported that the move of the Spirit was so overpowering that the floor was strewn with the bodies of people who had fallen under the power of God. One observer said that when the Spirit of the Lord fell, some people began to jerk, while others danced, wept, laughed, ran, shouted, and sang beautiful, heavenly songs unto the Lord. Our forefathers knew how to have a real, heartfelt Holy Ghost revival.

Brother Rodney also related that in many of the meetings of Charles Finney, the great revivalist, people would suddenly begin to wail at the top of their lungs. During one particular service, Brother Finney reportedly shouted to the crowd, "Be quiet. You're not in hell yet." They just wouldn't be quiet.

Finally, they had wailed so long and so loudly that Brother Finney walked over to an empty fireplace, stuck his head inside, and covered his mouth with a handkerchief because he was laughing uncontrollably with an indescribable joy. That's the way many of his mighty revivals would break out.

Brother Rodney also described how in the days of John Wesley's famous camp meetings, the horses would often come under the power of the Lord, and they would gallop for many miles at breakneck speed, taking their riders directly to the camp meeting.

Brother Rodney proclaimed, "This is not new. It might be new to you, but it's not new. It has been around as long as the Holy Ghost has been around. Whenever the Holy Ghost walks in the door, there's going to be an upheaval. Whenever the Holy Ghost walks in the door, man loses control and God takes control.

"You can come down, you can roll on the floor, you can be carried out, but if you don't allow the Holy Ghost to change you, you're going to stay the same as you were before the service. You've got to allow the Spirit of God to do a work deep within your heart. If you don't allow the Holy Ghost to change you, you are nothing more than a clanging cymbal and a noisy gong."

Brother Rodney stressed that no revival or outpouring of the Spirit should be judged by its outward manifestations. It must be judged by its fruit. He declared, "What is the fruit of the people's lives when they come out of that encounter with God? If they're not a better person, then I question whether or not it is of God."

Chapter 13

The Joy of the Lord Is Your Strength

When the joy of the Lord came into my life, it was like a great torrent of Holy Ghost power came flooding up in me, surging from the very depths of my soul. A mighty, sovereign move of the Spirit swept over my whole being like a powerful, rushing wind from heaven.

This Holy Ghost joy and laughter hit my life in much the same way that it must have hit the disciples of Jesus on the Day of Pentecost. Acts 2:1-4 declares that they were gathered in the Upper Room, when suddenly they were engulfed by the sound of a mighty rushing wind from heaven, and the Spirit of God descended upon them in the form of cloven tongues of fire. They were all filled with the Holy Ghost and began to speak with other tongues as the Spirit of God gave them utterance.

Devout men of every nation were dwelling in Jerusalem at that time, and when the power of God burst forth like a tidal wave from the Upper Room, the multitudes were confounded because they heard those men speaking in their own languages.

There were Parthians, Medes, Elamites, those from Mesopotamia, from Judea, from Cappadocia, from Pontus—in other words, from all the regions of the known world of that day. Those foreigners were gathered in Jerusalem for the great harvest festival, when suddenly they heard the disciples of Jesus, the men from Galilee, speaking in the dialects of the foreigners' native lands.

Then Peter, who was no doubt bubbling over with the Holy Ghost, stood to his feet and proclaimed, "These are not drunken, as ye suppose, since it is but the third hour of the day [nine o'clock in the morning]. But this is that which was spoken by the prophet Joel; and it shall come to pass in the last days, saith God, I will pour out my Spirit upon all flesh: and your sons and your daughters shall prophesy, and your young men shall see visions, and your old men shall dream dreams" (Acts 2:15-17 KJV).

When those men of faith burst forth from the Upper Room on the Day of Pentecost, the whole world thought they were drunk. Peter had to announce to the multitude which had gathered, "These men haven't been drinking alcohol. After all, it's only nine o'clock in the morning, and the Jerusalem bars aren't open yet. No, they're drunk on the new wine of the Spirit."

Going Forth in the Power of God

There's a fresh new move of the Spirit across America today, and God is once again restoring His holy joy and laughter to the church. We're beginning to draw water from the wells of salvation, and we're doing it with great joy. (Isa. 12:3.) Oh, that every born-again believer would receive a fresh baptism of the joy of the Lord and that it would come upon them suddenly, like it came into my life and the lives of those disciples in Jerusalem.

Why do I believe so strongly that we must have a fresh baptism of Holy Ghost joy? Because much of the body of Christ today is beaten down in their spirits. They feel disheartened and downtrodden because of the troubles and heartaches of life. Their heads are down and they feel subservient to the world. It seems as if the devil has trampled them in the dust. They've been whipped by Satan and all of his demons, and they're just waiting for the next deadly missile to come ripping through their lives. Many don't have a strong witness for the Lord because they have no joy. I know exactly how they feel because when this Holy Ghost laughter exploded in my life, I was a man who had no joy.

I had sunk so low that I'd almost forgotten Nehemiah 8:10, "The joy of the Lord is your strength." No wonder I felt like I was at the bottom of the barrel. I had no joy, so I had no strength. The Bible also says in Ephesians 6:10, "Be strong in the Lord [be empowered through your union with Him]; draw your strength from Him [that strength which His boundless might provides]" (AMP). It dawned on me that there was no way I could be strong in the Lord unless I was full of the joy of the Lord, which is my strength.

Can you imagine a heavyweight boxing champion going into the ring for a championship fight lying flat on his back in a hospital room with IVs hooked up to his body, having blood drawn every day, and running every imaginable test on him? Finally, after two weeks in the hospital, they release him only hours before he is scheduled to take on one of his leading contenders in a world championship title bout. What on earth would he do? I imagine any fighter in that position would postpone the fight until his strength could be renewed.

Many Christians today are staggering out onto the battlefield of life, desperately trying to rally for one last stand for Christ. They'll never be able to stand tall for Jesus without the joy of the Lord.

Isaiah 40:31 declares, "They that wait upon the Lord shall renew their strength; they shall mount up with wings as eagles; they shall run, and not be weary; and they shall walk, and not faint" (KJV). The key to those remarkable verses lies in waiting upon the Lord. As you wait on the Lord, and as you linger in His presence, you're going to find yourself overflowing with the joy of the Lord, because in His presence there is fullness of joy. (Ps. 16:11.) That's what this fresh baptism of joy is all about.

The Lord said in John 15:11 that He wants our joy to be full. Not just a weak little halfhearted trickle of joy bubbling up in our souls every now and then. Not just a tiny splashing stream of Holy Ghost joy and laughter flowing through our lives occasionally. But a mighty rushing river of the joy of the Lord pouring through our being every day of our lives. That is what the Lord desires for us.

Proverbs 17:22 says, "A happy heart is a good medicine and a cheerful mind works healing..." (AMP). There are some doctors today who will tell you, "If I can get a patient's spirit up, he or she has a much better chance of fully recovering." There are some hospitals in this country where they'll actually invite a comedian into the patients' rooms just to try to make them laugh. Why? Because even the secular world understands that laughter boosts your spirit. Even the medical profession has grasped that a merry heart, a heart full of joy and laughter, works like a powerful medicine.

The rest of that verse in Proverbs 17:22 declares, "...a broken spirit dries up the bones." Have you ever met someone who is as dry and brittle as a bone? I mean, they're so negative that when they walk into a room, it feels like somebody got up and walked out. Someone like that is a candidate for a fresh baptism of the joy of the Lord.

We see in Proverbs 15:15 that "all the days of the desponding afflicted are made evil [by anxious thoughts and foreboding], but he who has a glad heart has a continual feast [regardless of circumstances]" (AMP).

Notice that this Scripture does not deny the fact that negative circumstances exist. There are some people in the world today who try to deny the reality of negative circumstances, insisting that that's real faith. No, that's denial. I never deny that Satan is my adversary or that he's roaming this earth as a roaring lion, seeking whom he may devour. (1 Peter 5:8.) I just let that mighty river of joy come flooding up in my soul, which gives me the strength to stand against the devil and command him to flee.

Count It All Joy

The apostle James added another dimension to this subject of Holy Ghost joy when he wrote in James 1:2-4 (AMP):

> Consider it wholly joyful, my brethren, whenever you are enveloped in or encounter trials of any sort or fall into various temptations. Be assured and understand that the trial and proving of your faith brings out endurance and steadfastness and patience. But let endurance and stead-fastness and patience have full play and do a thorough work, so that you may be [people] perfectly and fully developed (with no defects), lacking in nothing.

I had no earthly idea how to count it all joy when I was engulfed by that mind-boggling avalanche of bills and debt. You could say that I hadn't really locked in on the Scripture. I had grasped what the apostle James meant when he talked about being enveloped in various trials and tribulations. I knew I was facing the fiercest opposition of my life, but I couldn't imagine how to count it all joy.

What a difference it made when that fresh baptism of Holy Ghost joy and laughter swept over my life. I could feel the joy bubbling up in my soul, even when it looked as though I were hurtling over the edge of a cliff. Almost the instant I arrived back in Tulsa after that fateful trip to Lakeland, Florida, the devil decided to throw a test at me. Isn't it amazing how, when something good happens, Satan always seems to show up on your doorstep, sneering at you, saying, "We'll see if this thing is real or not."

The test cropped up in the middle of one of our financial meetings when the telephone rang, and one of my associates answered it. "We need nearly $100,000 to pay for the university's insurance, and we've got to wire the money by two o'clock this afternoon," he said. In the natural, I knew what this meant. We had not been able to pay this particular bill for some time. The company had given us a final deadline. Unless we paid it, our entire insurance would be cancelled that day. However, when I received this word, I burst into a fit of Holy Ghost laughter. The man who had answered the phone was absolutely certain that I had lost it.

Let me remind you, I am a person who is usually in control. I simply do not break down laughing at problems of that magnitude—especially when they're due by two o'clock the same afternoon. But in the next split second, I was laughing so hard that I slid out of my chair and landed in a heap in the middle of the floor. That's where I was glued for at least five more minutes, laughing uncontrollably with the joy of the Lord.

As God is my witness, it was no more than twenty minutes later when the telephone rang, and the same man answered the phone. All of a sudden, his face turned as white as a sheet. "Richard," he blurted out, "you're not going to believe this, but we just got a check in the mail for $243,000." I fell out of my chair again, laughing hysterically in the Spirit.

Suddenly, everyone in the room was laughing with me. You could feel the gut-wrenching pressure being released. All at once my associates knew that the joy was real, and we had a hallelujah Jericho victory march around the conference table.

Before I received that fresh baptism of joy, there's no way I could have mustered up even a weak smile or a halfhearted chuckle when my associate gave me that shattering piece of news. I would have been the one turning as white as a sheet. God has filled me with His supernatural power to laugh even when Satan is shooting his biggest guns at me. I'm learning how to count it all joy even when it looks like the devil has the upper hand.

Joy Works

My mind flashes back to another moment when we were all gathered around that same conference table, facing a monstrous pile of bills, with absolutely no money to pay them. As we began to pray, instead of an atmosphere of gloom and doom, there was a buoyancy in our spirits and an unshakable expectancy for miracles. Out of the blue, a man walked into my office and declared, "God has told me to give you a million dollars."

I had never breathed a word about those staggering needs to anyone. But when that man handed me his million-dollar check, I felt so high in the Lord that I literally fell off my couch, laughing hilariously in the Spirit. I was speechless. Why? Because I was filled to overflowing with joy unspeakable and full of glory.

It was only a month or two later when that same man showed up at my office again with some more wonderful news: "God has told me to give you another million dollars." And several months after that he called me again, saying, "God has told me to give you another million dollars." Every time I was greeted with some more thrilling news, I found myself laughing spontaneously, uncontrollably—filled with a spirit of Holy Ghost joy.

I thank God for that man's obedient spirit, but if I hadn't received the joy of the Lord, I don't believe I could have stayed under the victory cloud of God. If I had been frantic, just beside myself with fear, God's heavenly supply line might have been cut off. When God poured out the joy of the Lord in my heart, He flung His heavenly supply line wide open.

While I was counting it all joy, taking my Holy Ghost joy medicine every day, one by one God was sweeping those forbidding mountains right out of my path. It wasn't long until I received a call from a man representing a company in Oklahoma City. He said that his company wanted to forgive a $500,000 debt against ORU. He told me, "Mr. Roberts, God has spoken to my heart, and I want to change the $500,000 debt to an outright contribution to Oral Roberts University." I was absolutely speechless.

During that same time period, the owner of a company in Florida, to whom ORU owed $60,000, heard that I was scheduled to preach in that state. He contacted me, saying, "Richard, I would like to meet with you." I knew we didn't have the $60,000 we owed him, but somehow I managed to scrape together $10,000 to give him as a gesture of good faith, hoping he would continue to carry the balance.

After I presented that man with our check, he said, "Richard, my wife and I have a great love for ORU, and we want our children to attend college there. We've prayed about this and would like to make the rest of ORU's $60,000 debt a direct contribution to the university." I began laughing with the joy of the Lord. That's exactly what God had said would happen while I watched Him pay off our debt.

Not long after that, there was another company to whom the university owed $470,000. By the grace of God, we were able to negotiate an arrangement with them to pay $55,000 in cash, along with loaning them some historic videos which our ministry owned, and they wiped out the entire debt. We received over $1 million in debt forgiveness.

I have evidence that the joy of the Lord works. I've got living proof that God's holy joy and laughter can break you free from Satan's snare. Before I received this happy, hilarious joy, I was getting beaten up in just about every area of my life, desperately wishing I could step over into God's stream of blessing. Now I have broken loose from that hellish bondage, and I'm marching on to victory in the Promised Land.

A Fresh Spirit of Joy

After that mighty revival of joy hit the ORU campus in 1993, our Board of Regents met for its regular fall meeting. The whole campus was vibrating with a fresh spirit of joy and holy laughter. One evening several of our board members were the guests of Lindsay and me on the TV program. Here's what they had to say about this extraordinary new baptism of Holy Ghost joy.

First of all, Karl Strader, pastor of Carpenter's Home Church in Lakeland, Florida, shared this testimony of the incredible outpouring of joy which had exploded in his church:

There were about five hundred churches that "crashed our party" with the Holy Ghost. The power of God fell all over the place, and people were filled with holy laughter. Between seven thousand and eight thousand people gave their hearts to the Lord in our church alone. People who were carrying heavy burdens found their burdens being lifted. Why? Because the kingdom of God is not meat and drink; it's righteousness and peace and joy in the Holy Ghost. (Rom. 14:17.)

A couple of our elders who were in the revival meetings left to go on a world preaching tour. The first country they visited was Russia. If anybody has had any reason to be depressed and downtrodden, it's the Russians, because even though communism had lifted, they didn't know what was going to happen tomorrow. Many Russian people don't laugh. They have nothing to laugh about. But in those meetings, 99 percent of the people were on the floor, stacked like cordwood, laughing hysterically.

Those same elders then went to Manila, where their children are missionaries. One told his father, "Dad, these people will not laugh. Asians don't respond that way." Everybody in the church fell to the floor under the power. They were laughing all over the place. The same thing happened in Singapore. Then the elders went to Uganda, Kenya, and several other African countries, and wherever they went, the same thing happened.

I believe this revival is the beginning of something that's going to sweep around the world. As the forces of evil are increasing everywhere, God is

125

lifting up a standard, and we're going to see a mighty tidal wave of revival upon this earth.

I want you to read what Marilyn Hickey, chairman of the Board of Regents of ORU, had to say about the way this amazing Holy Ghost revival of joy has affected her life. Marilyn and her husband, Wally, pastor Orchard Road Christian Center in Denver, Colorado:

> *Rodney Howard-Browne was in Denver for three weeks, and the first night I went, I saw people laughing, people falling [under the power], but I just sat there and cried. I knew it was real. I didn't understand what was going on, but I was so hungry for the manifested presence of God. I can't say that I was dry or depressed, but I was just hungry for God.*
>
> *My daughter, Sarah, came into town, and I told her, "I'm going over to Calvary Temple Sunday night. If you want to go, it's fine; but it's a little wild for you." She was very conservative back then, but she still decided to go. When Rodney came past us and said, "Receive the joy of the Lord," she fell into my lap laughing, and then I fell laughing into the lap of some stranger beside me.*
>
> *The next night when the service was over, we started walking out the door. She took my hand, and I fell to the floor laughing. She fell, too, and people couldn't get out the door without walking over us. I said, "I know about being the doorkeeper in the house of the Lord, but I haven't been a doormat before."*
>
> *For me, this experience was like renewing my first love. When you first meet Jesus, He's so precious to you, and His presence is so real. Well, that's what this was like. It was refreshing. It was like going on vacation. When the meetings were over, I loved people with a new love. I felt such compassion for them. We think joy does only one thing—it makes you laugh. But when God moves on us, He does what we need Him to do.*

Dr. John Hagee, pastor of Cornerstone Church in San Antonio, Texas, delivered a very powerful word on the joy of the Lord:

> *Solomon wrote in Proverbs that "a merry heart doeth good like a medicine" (Prov. 17:22 KJV). Jesus is the Great Physician, and He knows the medicine the soul needs when it's weary in well doing. God is giving His Bride a merry heart for a very depressing time.*

Forty years ago, no one would ever have believed that we would live in a nation of drive-by shootings, condoms in the schools, prayer and the Bible being taken out of the schools. Everything that we hold dear has been debased. The church has been under relentless attack. It is warfare of immeasurable intensity, and the only relief from that is the joy of the Lord.

On the other hand, there is no such thing as absolute euphoria every day of your life. Calvary was not a euphoric experience. Gethsemane was not a euphoric experience. After it was over, it produced joy unspeakable.

Life is not wonderful every day in the world. There's an enduring element here that the body of Christ must grasp. You have to punch it through and stay steady and let God help you get it into the end zone. When you get it into the end zone, then you can have your victory dance.

The fruit of the laughter is so very critical. There is a cult in Japan called the "laughter cult," and they go to the temple, flagellate themselves with roses, and laugh hysterically. The end result of their laughter is emptiness. It is one thing to laugh to become happy; it is another thing to laugh because you are happy. One is a psychic phenomenon; one is caused by the Holy Ghost.

We are experiencing something of the Holy Ghost because it glorifies the Father. It's bringing families together, giving divine relief, and giving us the strength to go on. For years, I have incorporated humor in my own ministry because it is one of the only things that will bring relief to people who are suffering.

One of the devil's trump cards is to tell you that if you come to Jesus, you can never have another happy day, you'll never do anything that's fun again, and your happy life is over. You don't know what happiness is until you find the Lord. He is the source of joy itself.

I want you to know that you can be happy in an unhappy world. Happiness is a matter of choice. You can be happy in political oppression. You can be happy when the government is taxing you immeasurably and taking your civil rights from you. You can be happy in the darkest storm of your life. Why? Because Jesus Christ is there.

Our dear friend, Billy Joe Daugherty, pastor of Victory Christian Center in Tulsa, Oklahoma, opened his heart and shared a very penetrating word about the joy of the Lord:

One of the things that has blessed me through the years has been the revelation that God never changes. It doesn't matter what the circumstances are or what your feelings are, His Word is going to come through. It never alters.

Our feelings of joy or feelings of sadness are triggered by thoughts. When people start thinking good things, the joy starts exploding in their lives. You can start thinking, I am redeemed from the curse. I am delivered. All things are working together for good. And joy starts getting all over you.

Another thing about joy is that when you reach out to people who are hurting—when you "send portions unto them for whom nothing [has been] prepared" (Neh. 8:10 KJV)—then the joy of the Lord will be your strength.

The Bible also says that a merry heart does you good like a medicine. Some people need to take the "God pill," and then a lot of things will begin to open up to them. John 7:38 KJV declares that out of your "belly shall flow rivers of living water." Joy flows out of the spirit, revelation flows out of it, and healing flows out of it. That's why Proverbs 4:23 says to guard your heart (your spirit) with all diligence.

Now there's another aspect of the joy as we explore all of these areas. Jesus said that there is joy in heaven over one sinner who repents. (Luke 15:10.) This is the hour of the greatest harvest. We understand that it's a time of the greatest darkness the earth has ever seen, but simultaneously it is a time of the greatest harvest. That means there is going to be more joy in this hour.

Before the TV program was over, Pastor Strader added one final word concerning why we, as Christians, have an absolutely unshakable reason to rejoice. He said, "If we have nothing else to laugh about, we ought to be rejoicing exceedingly, with great joy, because our names are written in the Lamb's book of life." As Christians, we, above all people on the face of this earth, have every reason to rejoice with unspeakable joy.

No Hangovers From the New Wine

Pastor Hagee put his finger on a key issue when he pointed out why he incorporates humor into his own ministry. He said, "It is one of the only things that will bring relief to people who are suffering." Not only does joy-filled, Holy Ghost laughter bring an indescribable release from your suffering, but the joy of the Lord has produced in my life what I call "Holy Ghost numbness." That may not sound very appealing to you, but let's explore this a little bit further.

When holy joy and laughter begin to flood through your being, it's like taking a strong dose of medicine to help numb you to the problem. When some people are struck by a terrible tragedy, they may decide to get bombed out of their minds on liquor. Why? Because they're trying to numb themselves to their problems. People have drunk themselves into a drunken stupor just to escape from their troubles. You can get a brutal hangover from that kind of numbness, but there's no hangover from the joy of the Lord!

The joy of the Lord is so refreshing that I've been drinking down at "Joel's place" lately—the prophet Joel's place, that is. I've been drinking from those rivers of living water, the wells of salvation that never run dry. I've been drinking from the fountain where God's joy is overflowing, and there's nothing else in the world like it.

Chapter 14

A Laughing or a Crying Revival: Your Choice

There has been some criticism from certain church leaders who have called this move of God the "laughing revival." I want to ask one question: "Would you rather have a crying revival?" Haven't we all cried enough tears, like the old country-and-western songs say: "I Get Tears in My Beer," or, "Baby, You Done Sorta Stepped on My Aorta"?

Aren't you tired of crying? Wouldn't you rather have the joy of the Lord in your heart than a bucketful of tears? Or would you rather be melancholy? Maybe we should stop calling our churches the "Happy Church" or the "Victorious Church." Perhaps we should start calling them something like the "Growling Church," or the "Grumbling Church," or the "First Church of the Weeping Willow." If you'd rather have a permanent frown on your face, I'm not knocking it. The frown, however, wasn't working for me. Neither were the ulcer and sleepless nights. I had to have something fresh. I needed a revolutionary change in my life.

I was flabbergasted when a minister friend of mine turned me down flat after I invited him to one of Brother Rodney Howard-Browne's services. He informed me that he could not support me in this revival of joy, and he would not come. Then he added, "I have a philosophical objection to the emphasis on laughter." And I thought to myself, *Well, would you rather have an emphasis on frowning?* But I replied, "The emphasis isn't on laughter. The emphasis is on revival. The emphasis is on repentance and on changed lives."

When I tell people that the joy of the Lord saved my life, I mean exactly that. The *laughter* did not save my life; it was the joy of the Lord that lifted me out of the devil's quagmire, and I had been sinking fast. Laughter is not the mainstream of this move of God's Spirit. It's merely a by-product. It's an outward manifestation of what's happening on the inside of your innermost being. The mainstream is a changed heart.

Even though I was jolted by this minister's reaction, I went on to relate to him a most unusual experience I'd had during the revival at ORU. I'm not a person who weeps easily. When Brother Rodney laid hands on me during one of the services, I fell to the floor under the power of God, and the Holy Spirit came upon me so strongly that I began to weep and shake and sob uncontrollably.

While I was lying on the floor, broken before the Lord, God gave me an astonishing vision in my spirit. In a moment, I saw the debt at ORU completely wiped away. I saw our endowment soaring and the enrollment bursting at the seams. I saw the students in the years to come streaming to the four corners of the earth with the healing Gospel of Jesus. In the flash of a second, I saw it all.

I've talked about the day when ORU will be out of debt, and I've clung fiercely to my faith that we will reach that goal. But for the very first time, a picture flashed through my mind of what I had been saying with my mouth. When I had this vision, it literally tore me up.

Then I heard the Lord whispering in my heart, *Now that you've seen what you've only spoken of before, you can decree it into being, and what you saw will happen.* I then made a fresh vow to the Lord to see that ORU never departs from its founding purpose.

During that same service, Brother Rodney laid hands on our daughter Olivia, and she told us later, "The Lord said to me, 'When you grow up, you're going to preach.'" That touched a strong chord in my heart. This move of the Spirit is changing lives. It's a true heaven-opening, hell-shaking Holy Ghost move of God's spirit.

After I told this minister about my experience, I exclaimed, "If you owed $56 million, you'd want the joy of the Lord in your life, too."

There are some people who don't want to put their big toe into God's "suddenly." I don't want to merely dip my big toe into the water. I want to dive down deep into the flow of God's Spirit. I want to be ready at a moment's notice to move with the victory cloud of God.

Correctly Judging the Spirit

There's another hurdle that some people have to get over before they can dive into the river of God's joy. Some have expressed the feeling that this Holy Ghost laughter seems to be fake. They believe that some people are getting over into the flesh with the joy of the Lord. Even if that is true, that doesn't mean that you and I can get by without a full dose of the joy of the Lord. As a preacher friend of mine once said, "I'd rather have a little wildfire than no fire at all."

No doubt there are some who are getting over into the flesh with this brand-new move of the Spirit, but we are flesh. I believe it's far more dangerous to stifle the move of God simply because a few people get into the flesh. I'd rather deal with those few on an individual basis and help them see to flow correctly with the Holy Spirit. There should be some admonition and teaching in this area, along with the moving of the Spirit, but let's not throw the baby out with the bathwater.

Cutting Out the Red Tape

This happy, hilarious, Holy Ghost laughter wasn't the only result of this outpouring of joy in my life. The joy of the Lord brought a remarkable change in me, a real reviving of my entire life. It was like the Bible says in Isaiah 43:18-19. God caused a river of joy to spring up in the middle of a scorching wasteland. He caused the parched, thirsty desert of my life to blossom like a rose. (Isa. 35:1.)

Not only has *my* life been transformed, but this extraordinary explosion of holy joy and laughter has been spreading around the world. It's bringing a dramatic change in churches everywhere. In Great Britain, this move of the Holy Spirit has come into many churches. It's bringing old-time revival and repentance into people's hearts. It's bringing wholeness and holiness, and an incredible outpouring of signs and wonders, healing, and miracles.

One of the most gratifying by-products of the joy of the Lord in my life was holy laughter from heaven. I've truly been laughing a lot. I attended another meeting at Rhema Bible Church, and Brother Kenneth Hagin, Sr., said to me, "You know, I don't understand all this confusion about people who laugh. When you're happy, you laugh. What's so hard to understand about that?"

I've seen some people in these amazing revival services who didn't utter even a single chuckle. Some react the way Marilyn Hickey did at that first meeting she attended in Denver. She was so overcome by the awesome presence of the Lord that she just wept and wept. Her experience is not an isolated one. I've seen countless numbers of people in these Holy Ghost meetings with tears rolling down their cheeks—tears of joy, repentance, and cleansing. For me, the revival at ORU was an experience of weeping uncontrollably in the presence of the Lord.

Didn't the psalmist David declare, "Purge me with hyssop.... Create in me a clean heart, O God"? (Ps. 51:7,10). David stumbled headlong into a pit of sin when he committed adultery with Bathsheba. But he cried out to the Lord, "Wash me thoroughly from my iniquity, and cleanse me from my sin" (Ps. 51:2). I believe that cleansing His people from their sins is one of the things God has been doing through this revolutionary outbreak of Holy Ghost joy.

Sometimes I find myself being engulfed with happy, uncontainable, joy-filled laughter, and I find myself weeping in the awesome presence of the Lord. But after the laughter and after the weeping, I always find myself changed in the depths of my soul. The Lord is cutting through all of the red tape in my life. He is lifting me up to serve Him with a mighty spirit of joy.

Chapter 15

Step Out of Your Comfort Zone

When you *want* something you've never had before, you must *do* something you've never done before. You must break free from your comfort zone and launch out toward your miracle with a mighty leap of faith. Even though you may find yourself in a never-ending difficult situation, you have to guard that you don't get used to the difficulties; instead of continuing to stand against them in faith, you allow them to become a permanent fixture in your life.

In Matthew 12, there's a dramatic scene where the Lord Jesus Christ called a man out of his comfort zone. The Bible says that Jesus was conducting a great miracle service in the synagogue when all of a sudden He glanced up and saw a man who had a withered hand.

Now when He [Jesus] had departed from there, He went into their synagogue.

And behold, there was a man who had a withered hand. And they asked Him, saying, "Is it lawful to heal on the Sabbath?"—that they might accuse Him.

Then He said to them, "What man is there among you who has one sheep, and if it falls into a pit on the Sabbath, will not lay hold of it and lift it out?

Of how much more value then is a man than a sheep? Therefore it is lawful to do good on the Sabbath."

Then He said to the man, "Stretch out your hand." And he stretched it out, and it was restored as whole as the other.

MATTHEW 12:9-13

Luke's narrative of this incident says that the man's right hand was withered. (Luke 6:6.) Your right hand represents your hand of strength. It's your hand of power. Most people in the world are right-handed, so when Jesus Christ saw that this man had a withered right hand, He understood more about the man's emotional and spiritual condition as well.

The Lord Jesus Christ knows the condition you're in right now. He knows who you are and where you live. He knows what you're going through. He sees your struggles, turmoil, and heartache.

The religious leaders decided to ask Jesus a trick question. They were trying to trap and accuse Him of a crime, so they posed a cunning question to Him. They asked, "Is it right to heal on the Sabbath days?" Jesus knew the wickedness of their hearts. He cut through their smoke screen and replied, "Which one of you has a sheep? And should it fall into a pit on the Sabbath, would you not go and rescue it from the pit?" (Matt. 12:11.)

It's so easy for someone to fall into a pit. David was a man who found himself "in a pit," hiding in a cave to escape the javelin of King Saul. (1 Sam. 24:3.) Joseph also was cast into a pit, thrown there by his very own brothers. (Gen. 37:24.) The prophet Jeremiah was also trapped in a pit. Evil men threw him into a dungeon because he refused to stop prophesying. (Jer. 38:6.) Daniel was also cast into a pit—a lions' den—because he prayed to the Lord. But God sent His angel into that den and padlocked the lions' jaws. (Dan. 6:22.)

God delivered each one of these saints from their pits through His miraculous power. I have news for you. You may have stumbled head-long into the devil's pit, but I believe God will bring you out.

Is Your Pit Your Comfort Zone?

Pits are terrible things. They are what I call the "nowhere zone." The nowhere zone is when you're halfway between where you were and where you want to be. A nowhere zone is another name for a comfort zone. As long as you stay in your comfort zone, you are going nowhere.

Jesus Christ realized that the man with the withered hand had fallen into a pit of infirmity, and the pit had become his comfort zone. You see, no doubt the man became comfortable with his infirmity. He had grown accustomed to his withered hand.

What does it mean when we say something is withered? It means that it lacks moisture and has dried up. It isn't supple and flexible. Many of us today have dryness, or a lack of moisture, in our lives. We lack the moisture of the "rivers of living water" Jesus promises us in John 7:38.

When something is withered in your life, you don't want to be out in front of the crowd. You want to hide in the shadows. Oftentimes you're embarrassed by the problem, and you hide it behind your back. You try to muster up a smile because you don't want anybody to know that something is wrong.

Oh, the "withered hands" of life. A withered hand can be anything that's troubling you. It can be sin, faults, or shortcomings that continually trip you up. It can be a devastating setback or a shameful secret from your past. It can be a crippling, death-dealing disease, a fear, a nagging doubt, or some other satanic attack of the devil. But Jesus Christ is saying to us today, "It's time to stretch out your withered hand and make a move toward God."

Perhaps this man was cowering in the back of the room, trying to vanish into the shadows, when Jesus Christ called him out of the crowd, saying, "Arise and stand here" (Luke 6:8). I believe He was telling the man, "Come out of the darkness. Come out of your comfort zone. Come out of the back row of life."

Then the Lord said to him, "Stretch out your hand." How on earth could he stretch out his hand when it was limp and useless? In the natural, there was no way he could reach out. Yet, this is precisely what Jesus commanded him to do.

An incident stands out in my mind that clearly illustrates this. Some years ago I was preaching in Calgary, Alberta, Canada, and a man who had suffered from agonizing back problems for twenty years came forward for prayer. Instead of laying my hands on him, I simply said, "My brother, bend over three times."

"I can't bend over," he blurted out. "That's why I came for prayer."

He resisted me because I asked him to step out of his comfort zone. Once again I repeated, "Please bend over three times." He rolled his eyes at me as if he thought I were from another world.

Then, very reluctantly, he started to bend over. The first time he tried he couldn't bend down very far. He looked at me as if to say, "See, I told you so."

"Bend over a second time," I insisted. The second time he could bend over a little farther. The third time he bent down to the floor.

In utter shock and amazement, he looked up at me and exclaimed, "What did you do?"

"I didn't do anything," I replied.

I believe God healed that man because he broke free from his comfort zone. God wants us to abandon our safe little comfort zones as well and launch out in a great leap of faith toward Him.

I believe Jesus is saying to you today, "Stand forth. Stretch out your withered hand." Yes, it may be difficult, and there may be people who will try to hinder you. There may be some who will tell you that God has lost His power, that He cannot restore your withered hand. Who are you going to believe? Are you going to believe the Bible, or will you trust in what the world says?

Jesus told the man to stretch out his hand; and as the man obeyed, the healing power of God surged through his hand and he was made whole. It made the religious people mad, but it made Jesus glad. And I believe that if you will stretch out your hand—your faith—God will move on the scene with a mighty outpouring of His power, which will enable you to get out of your comfort zone and receive the miracle you so desperately need.

The What-Ifs of Life

From Genesis to Revelation, the Bible is packed with stories of men and women who had to step out of their comfort zones before they could receive a miracle. I wonder what would have happened if they had balked at the will of God and refused to move?

For example, what would have happened if Noah had refused to budge from his comfort zone when God commanded him to build the ark? (Gen. 6.) What if Noah had started whining to the Lord, "What's rain? And what's a boat?" You see, in Noah's day it had never rained before the Flood.

What if Noah had asked God, "What do You mean, build an ark? Build it *how* high?" Or, "*Why* do You want me to gather my family and a male and female of all the animals and load them onto the ark?" What if he had stopped halfway through the construction of the ark because the people were mocking him? What if they told him to get that ark out of the street because it's an eyesore to the whole neighborhood?

What if Noah had refused to step out of his comfort zone? I'll tell you what if. He and his family would have been wiped out with the rest of mankind in the Flood. They would have been drowned with the ungodly, and God would have had to find another way to save a righteous remnant. (Gen. 7.)

Let me ask you another question. What if Moses had refused to step out of his comfort zone and take off his shoes when God said, "Moses, you're standing on holy ground"? (Ex. 3:5.) What if he had refused to leave his old, familiar surroundings in the wilderness, where he had been wandering for forty years, a fugitive from Pharaoh? Or what if Moses had gone to Egypt as God had commanded him and called down the great plagues upon Pharaoh, but then decided he didn't want to smear blood on the doorposts as the Lord had instructed him to do? (Ex. 12.)

What if Moses had declared, "Now listen, God, by Your power I've turned the river of Egypt into blood; I've called down frogs, lice, flies, boils, hailstones, and locusts, but I really don't want to kill a lamb and smear its blood on the doorposts—that's going too far"? I'll tell you what if. The death angel wouldn't have passed over Israel. Not only would the firstborn of Egypt have perished that night, but all of the firstborn in Israel would have died as well.

Do you remember the story of David and Goliath? What if David, as a young shepherd, had refused to step out of his comfort zone? Can't you picture him, clutching the sandwiches he had brought to his brothers who were stationed on the front lines with King Saul? All of a sudden he sees Goliath strutting back and forth across the valley, casting a giant's shadow over the land. (1 Sam. 17.) What if David had cut and run, yelling, "Here, take your sandwiches; I've got to go"? Or what if he had proposed, "Okay, I'll fight the giant, but only if I can wear Saul's armor"?

I believe that if David had come out dressed in a suit of armor, Goliath wouldn't have had to lift his visor to laugh at the seventeen-year-old, ruddy-complexioned boy who was running toward him. David wouldn't have been running. He would have been crawling at a snail's pace, weighed down by armor that didn't fit.

If Goliath hadn't raised his visor, he never would have exposed his forehead, which was the only vulnerable spot on his whole body. If David had refused to come out of his comfort zone, that giant would have pulverized him, and the birds of the air would have had a good dinner.

What about the four starving lepers who sat at the gates of Samaria? They were stranded between a fortressed city and the enemy army that surrounded it. They could have sighed to each other, "Let's sit here until we die." (2 Kings 7.) What if, at twilight, as they pondered whether or not they should launch out on a great march of faith and surrender themselves to the mercies of their enemies, one had announced, "Brothers, I believe it's too dark for us to strike out on such a dangerous mission. And besides, who are we to try to face the enemy alone? We're the least likely ones to do the job." I'll tell you what if. Those men would have starved to death at the gates of the city.

What if Jesus had said no to God and refused to step out of His comfort zone? He had a good thing going—a miracle ministry and an enthusiastic following. He had every reason to live. Where would we be if Jesus had decided to call down a legion of angels to save Him instead of laying down His life? What if, in the Garden of Gethsemane, Jesus had cried out, "Father, I don't want to go to the Cross. I know it sounded like a good idea when I was with You in heaven, but now I'm not so sure about it"?

What if He had said, "God, I don't want to have My hands and feet nailed to a tree. I don't want to have a spear thrust into My side. This is as far as I'm going. I'm heading back to Nazareth to become a carpenter again"? I'll tell you what if. If Jesus hadn't gone to the Cross, you and I wouldn't be saved from our sins. We wouldn't be washed in the blood of the Lamb. We wouldn't have the opportunity to know Jesus Christ as our Lord and Savior.

God's Escape Hatch Out of Comfort Zones.

Every person mentioned did something radical when they stepped out of their comfort zones. Everybody has comfort zones, and we do not like to come out of them. Why? It's easier to stay in a comfort zone because there aren't any risks or hurdles to overcome.

Comfort zones are terrible bondages. They're boxes that are difficult to break out of because Satan will wrap them so tightly that you'll think there is no way out. Jesus has made a way for us to get out of the boxes the devil tries to trap us in. When our hope seems gone and we want to get out of the hell we're in, we have to break out of our comfort zones. If we step out by faith, I believe the Lord will launch us out to do great exploits for God.

Chapter 16

Listen to Good Reports

We're living in a time of great misery in the world. Famine and pestilence are sweeping the globe. Earthquakes are rocking the earth in unprecedented numbers. We've seen tidal waves like never before. You can hear bad reports blaring from your television set any time of the day or night. You can flip on a local radio station and listen to bad reports being pumped out across the airwaves.

It's heartrending to hear the news of a gruesome accident or to read about a desperate mother who has apparently murdered her own children or to listen to a TV commentator report on terrorism around the world. Listening to the news can be depressing. Wherever you look, it seems as if you're being bombarded by bad reports. The only way to make it through the hell you're going through is to stop listening to the bad reports and start listening to good reports.

In Numbers 13 and 14, the Bible paints a vivid picture of a group of people who listened to a bad report, and it cost them dearly. If you recall the story, after Moses had led the children of Israel out of Egyptian bondage, there only remained an eleven-day journey to the Promised Land. By the time the people had murmured and complained their way across the wilderness, it took them forty death-dealing years to make that trip. Why did it take them so long? Because they listened to a bad report.

After the Israelites had escaped from Pharaoh's armies, they crossed the wilderness until they stood at the very edge of the Promised Land.

The Lord told Moses to send twelve of his men—a leader from each tribe—to spy out the land. When the spies returned, ten of them brought back an alarming report. They said, "There are huge giants in the land. They're so gigantic that we look like grasshoppers in their sight."

As soon as the travel-weary Israelites heard the bad report, consternation swept through the camp. They began to weep and wail so loudly that Moses could scarcely quiet them. Really, they were furious with him. *The nerve of Moses, leading us to a land that is filled with giants.* Never mind the fact that the spies had brought back enormous clusters of grapes, huge pomegranates, and juicy figs from the rich countryside. The bounty of the land was staggering.

The Promised Land Is Yours

The other two spies, Joshua and Caleb, began to protest. "Don't be dismayed," they cried. "Yes, we saw how tall the giants were, but the land is a wonderful land, a land of plenty. The Lord is with us, and with His help, we're well able to go up and possess it." I want you to notice that Joshua and Caleb's good report made the children of Israel boiling mad—so mad that they talked about stoning them to death.

The most amazing thing to me about this whole story is the fact that all twelve spies searched out the same piece of land. They all saw the same giants. Each one of them encountered the same obstacles. They all saw the same clusters of grapes, the same bountiful fruit of the land. Nothing about the land had changed between the time Joshua and Caleb searched it out and the time the rest of the spies searched it out. It was the very same land.

How could ten spies bring back such a totally different report from Joshua and Caleb's report? It's very simple. The men who brought back the bad report were operating in fear. Joshua and Caleb, on the other hand, operated in faith.

When the giants of life loom up before you and you feel so small and helpless, I hope you'll remember this story. You can quiver and quake and rattle off the bad report, or you can choose to face the giants in faith. Joshua and Caleb chose to face them with their faith. They said, "The Lord is with us. Do not fear them" (Num. 14:9).

Just think about the awful penalty the children of Israel paid because they listened to the bad report. They wandered through the wilderness for forty years until every last one who had believed the bad report was dead. Listening to a bad report turned an eleven-day journey into a forty-year wilderness experience. I don't know about you, but I'll take the eleven-day journey any day.

Listening to the Devil's Report

I can't begin to describe the fear that swept over me when Satan first began to give me the bad reports about Oral Roberts University. He would tell me, "ORU is going under, and everybody is going to blame you. Can't you see the headline: 'Richard Roberts Takes Oral Roberts University Down the Tubes?' There will be nowhere for you to run and hide. Everyone will say, 'You allowed a great university to fall into ruins.'"

When I lay down to sleep at night, terrible nightmares stole my sleep. I would awaken in the middle of the night in a cold sweat, trying to shake off visions of the university going under. When I would finally drift off to sleep, many times I was jolted awake by visions of the awful imaginary newspaper headlines before my eyes: "Richard Roberts Takes ORU Down the Drain." In my mind's eye, I could see the authorities dismantling ORU and the doors being bolted shut.

Every morning when I went into the office, I was flooded with bad reports. The creditors and bankers seemed unanimous: There simply wasn't enough cash to meet all of our obligations.

It seemed that everyone who spied out the land for me came back with a deadly, negative report. I didn't want to wander in the wilderness for forty years, so I decided to listen to the good report. I did not bury my head in the sand and try to deny the facts. I'm not into denial. But you and I do not have to live by the facts alone. The Bible says, "The just shall live *by faith*" (Heb. 10:38).

I did not deny that there was a $56 million debt hanging over ORU like a cloud. I did not deny that as the President and Chief Executive Officer, I was responsible for that debt. I did not deny that it appeared we were going to have to close the doors of the university.

Standing Strong in Faith

My faith gave me a different report. My faith said, "I can do all things through Christ who strengthens me" (Phil. 4:13). My faith said, "Greater is he that is in you, than he that is in the world" (1 John 4:4 KJV). My faith declared, "My God always causes me to triumph in Christ" (2 Cor. 2:14). I decided to listen to the good report, and it forever changed my life.

When the naysayers and the gainsayers shouted their doom-and-gloom prophecies at me, I refused to listen to them. I ignored the boys over on the side of the road to Bethel who taunted me like the crowd who mocked Elisha about Elijah going up in the whirlwind. (2 Kings 2:23.)

There's probably an area of your life in which you have received a good and a bad report. The question is, Whose report are you going to believe?

A Promised Land lies before you, and it's divinely ordained to be yours. Your name has been stamped on it from the beginning of time. God Almighty has chosen you to go up and possess the land. To do so, you have to listen to the report of the Joshuas and Calebs of this life. You've got to listen to the report of God's Word.

We are well able to possess the land and take our cities for the Lord. We are well able to take our families, our neighborhoods, our schools, our workplaces. It's time for us to set our course for the Promised Land. We *can* prevail against hell and possess all of God's promises if we will only keep our focus on the good reports.

Chapter 17

The Right Attitude

When you tumble headlong into the middle of a hellish situation, it's absolutely vital for you to keep your attitude right. There are times in all of our lives when we need to make a Holy Ghost attitude adjustment. What do I mean by a Holy Ghost attitude adjustment? Well, perhaps you've been looking down, and you need to start looking up. Or maybe you need to bury the ghost of the past so you can launch out onto a fresh path in your life.

Jesus has told us that the only way to bury the ghost of the past is to call on the Holy Spirit. In John 7 the Lord gives us the Bible formula for making a Holy Ghost attitude adjustment. This scene takes place on the last great day of the Jewish Feast of Tabernacles, when Jesus did something which had never been done before. He did it in a rare and an emphatic way. Jesus broke all tradition when He stopped the processional and shouted:

> "If anyone thirsts, let him come to Me and drink.
> He who believes in Me, as the Scripture has said, out of his heart will flow rivers of living water."
> But this He spoke concerning the Spirit, whom those believing in Him would receive; for the Holy Spirit was not yet given, because Jesus was not yet glorified.
>
> JOHN 7:37-39

Jesus was saying, "If anyone is grappling with a problem, needs to make an attitude adjustment, or thirsts to get from where he is to where he wants to be, let him come to Me." God makes the answer so clear. It's so simple that it's profound.

This dramatic event took place before the outpouring of the Holy Spirit. Thank God, we're living in the day when the Spirit of God has already been poured out, and His Spirit does not need to be poured out a second time. He is where I am, and He's where you are. He's ready to flood your whole being with the wonder-working power of God.

If we want to make it through the hellish situations of life, we've got to plunge into the river of God's Spirit. If we want to leave the past behind and make a fresh, new start in our lives, we've got to learn how to open up the tap so the Spirit of God can flow through.

Back in the days of the Old West, when tragedy struck someone's life, he would simply jump on a horse or buy a ticket on the nearest stagecoach and relocate to some other town where he was not known. There were no televisions or radio stations, and most of the time no one would recognize him, and his name was usually not known. In the Old West, it was common to hear someone say that a cowboy was "riding with a secret." That meant there was something in his past that he wanted to overcome, so he was looking for a new place to start afresh.

Today is the time and place for you to start your life anew. You may be thinking, *Richard, you don't know my past*. While that's true, it's time to put the past in the past. It's time to bury the ghosts that have been haunting you and to call upon the Holy Spirit so you can start anew.

A lot of people today are walking around with a secret. A deep, dark secret may be lodged within your heart that nobody else knows about except you and God. You're wondering if life is ever going to be any different. It's only going to be different if you have an attitude adjustment by the power of God's Spirit.

The apostle Paul declared, "There's not one single thing I can do about the past. All I can do is give it to the Lord. Then I can lift my head up and press on toward the mark for the prize of the high calling of God in Christ Jesus." (Phil. 3:13,14.) There is a prize out there that's worth attaining. In order to lay hold of it, we're going to have to keep our attitudes right.

Learning How To Make Right Choices

Is God's spiritual river flowing in your life today? Are you being refreshed in the Spirit, or are you stale in the Spirit? Are you being filled with the Spirit, or are you thirsty, dry, and crusty on the inside? Are you free in the Spirit, or are you hindering the flow of God's Spirit? Are you overflowing in the Spirit, or are you stagnant in the Spirit?

Let me illustrate in geographical terms what I'm talking about. In the nation of Israel, the Sea of Galilee is a magnificent body of water, a huge inland lake that teems with life. Why? Because water flows freely into it and also gushes out of it. If you follow its main inlet and outlet, the Jordan River, to the place where it empties into the Dead Sea, you'll notice that the water pours in, but nothing pours out. That's why it's called dead. And because it's dead, it has a bad odor.

In the same way, some Christians smell bad because they're old, dry, and crusty in their spirits. We may be eighteen, forty-five, sixty-five, or any age on the outside, but we can still be old, dry, and crusty on the inside no matter what our physical age is.

Now, is anything jamming up the flow of God's Spirit in your life—things like unconfessed sin, pride, anger toward God or toward other people, unforgiveness, bitterness, depression, or just a general feeling of being down on yourself? You may be thinking, *Richard, I can't seem to get over this problem, this attitude.* No, you can't do it by yourself. You need the active, energizing power of the Holy Spirit to help you.

Jesus declared, "Are any of you thirsty? Are any of you dry, and you feel like you're about to have a crackup? Are you hurting? Alone? Troubled? Is there any sickness, heartache, loneliness? Are there money problems? Family problems? Relationship problems?" Then He added, "Come to Me and drink. Step into the river."

Why do I talk so much about the baptism of the Holy Spirit? The Holy Spirit—the divine Paraclete—is the only One who can empower you to overcome your problems. I pray in tongues—the prayer language of the Spirit—every day of my life because I need help. I'm hit with a barrage of decisions each day, and many times I don't have a clue as to what I should do. Aren't there times when you wish someone would tell you which path to take—to say, "Go this way," "Do this," or "Do that"?

Maybe there's a decision hanging out there in front of you, and your heart is tugging you in one direction, while your mind is pulling you in another direction. That's when the Holy Spirit comes in to help you make the right choice.

Tapping Into the Holy Spirit's Wisdom

Perhaps you were raised in a denomination that teaches against the baptism of the Holy Spirit. You may not be accustomed to praying in the Holy Spirit. One reason many people have reacted so negatively to the baptism of the Holy Spirit is the unfortunate way some Christians have presented it.

They have somehow given the false impression that the gift of tongues, which is one of the nine gifts of the Spirit described in 1 Corinthians 12, is the same thing as the daily devotional prayer language of the Spirit. They've mistakenly asked, "Do you have the gift of tongues?" Anyone who has a strong Bible background knows there is a big difference between the two. As a result, many people have been turned off by this discrepancy.

To the best of my knowledge, the gift of tongues has never operated in my life, but I pray in tongues, in the prayer language of the Spirit, every day of my life. The gifts of the Holy Spirit are sovereign manifestations of the Lord and are given only as the Spirit wills. No one can decide when and where the gifts of the Spirit will operate through his or her life.

I can't decide that I'm going to manifest the gift of tongues or that the gift of prophecy is going to operate through me. I can't produce the word of wisdom or the word of knowledge by an act of my human will. However, every born-again believer has a Bible right to tap in to the Holy Spirit's prayer. We can pray in our daily devotional prayer language any time we desire.

You may believe that speaking in tongues isn't for everybody, but Acts 2:39 proclaims that the gift of the Holy Ghost is given to you, and to your children, and to all that are afar off, even as many as the Lord our God shall call. If God has called you to be His child, then the gift of the Holy Spirit is for you. The apostle Paul also declared, "I would like every one of you to speak in tongues…" (1 Cor. 14:5 NIV). The baptism of the Holy Spirit is for every born-again believer.

Ask and Receive

It's not hard to receive this gift of the Holy Spirit. If you're a Christian, God's Spirit took up residence in your heart the day that you were born again. He bore witness with your spirit that you are a child of God. (Rom. 8:16.)

The Holy Spirit isn't residing in your heart having a party. He's not in your innermost being having a picnic. He's not in your spirit playing games. What is He doing? Romans 8:26-27 clearly states that He is interceding. He's praying seven days a week, twenty-four hours a day, on a straight line to the Lord. All you have to do is open your heart and tap in to the Spirit's prayer.

Some people have the mistaken idea that the Holy Spirit will somehow take control of their tongues and force them to speak, but nothing could be further from the truth. We have to stir up the gift of the Holy Spirit. We decide to pray in tongues by an act of our human will. The apostle Paul said, "I will [determine to] pray with the Spirit, and I will also pray [in my own language or] with [my] understanding" (1 Cor. 14:15). That means you can pray in the Spirit anytime you want to. Anytime in the day or nighttime, anytime you're happy or sad, anytime you feel up or down, anytime there's trouble or victory in your life, you can pray in tongues.

Praying in the Spirit isn't some strange, mystical experience that's designed for a few fanatics somewhere over on the fringe. It's one of the Bible doctrines God has given to the church. It's not something that's hard to grasp. It's simply you and me talking to our heavenly Father in a language that only He understands. It's praying out the mysteries of God, praying out His plans and purposes in our lives. (1 Cor. 14:2.)

It's time to stop trying to analyze the Holy Ghost and making a big theological statement out of the prayer language of the Spirit. It's time just to pray in the Spirit, and expect it to change your life dramatically. Praying in the Spirit is what will build you up as a Christian. Jude 20 NIV declares, "But you, dear friends, build yourselves up in your most holy faith and pray in the Holy Spirit."

I'm not trying to cram something down your throat, but I want you to get as much of God as you can get. What I want for you is all that God has for you. I don't want you to have half a loaf or go through life with the other half. I want you to get the whole loaf from the Spirit of God.

Step on out in the River

Perhaps you've never stepped into the river of God's Spirit. You may be afraid to speak in tongues. I remember one outstanding gospel singer who refused to appear as a guest on my television show. When I asked why, the reply came back, "Richard, you speak in tongues, and I'm afraid the Holy Spirit will say something to me and scare me to death, and my ministry will be wrecked."

It's sad that many Christians have been taught this way. But sadly enough, most of the church world today treats the Holy Spirit as if He is not even there. Yet, He's the One who will lead you and guide you on a daily basis if you'll only let Him.

I tell you, praying in tongues is what keeps my life together. When I first became president of ORU, I thought I would go out of my mind. I had never been strapped with a $56 million debt before, nor had I ever been responsible for educating thousands of young people. Without the baptism of the Holy Spirit and God revealing His strategy to me by His Spirit, I don't think I could have withstood the devil's onslaught. And I'm not the only one who has to withstand an onslaught. Satan wants to wreak havoc on God's plan for your life as well.

It's time for you to plunge into the river and to get into the flow of the mighty Holy Ghost. The water isn't cold. It's just the right temperature, and it's fresh and clear. It's not shallow either. It's deep. It's like that old song we used to sing, "Deep and Wide." It's a river flowing freely from the throne of God.

Jesus declared, "If any man is thirsty, if any woman is thirsty, if anyone is craving a change in his life, let them come to Me, and let them drink." (John 7:37.) It's time for every born-again child of God to be filled with the Spirit and pray in tongues. It's time for Christians everywhere to have a Holy Ghost attitude adjustment. Why don't you pitch everything that has hindered you out the window and step into the river of God's mighty Holy Ghost power and experience Him for yourself.

Chapter 18

Avoiding the Pitfalls the Second Time Around

Why is it that some people seem to get yanked back into the same old traps over and over again? They seem to be caught in a loop and can't get off. I don't believe anyone just leaps out of bed in the morning and exclaims, "Glory be to God, I believe I'll make a mistake today." That's not how it happens.

Most of the time people don't purpose in their hearts to make a mistake, but we've all made enough mistakes in our lifetimes to last forever. The big question is, Do we learn from our mistakes? Do we avoid the pitfalls the second time around, or do we simply stumble headlong into the same old snares again and again?

Time after time, we repeat the same mistakes in every arena of life. We've seen this type of pattern creep into the lives of officials in the highest levels of our government. We've seen it infiltrate many other walks of life. People slip into disgrace, and they publicly repent and promise, "I'll never do that again." But somehow, in their humanness, they wind up doing the same thing again, exactly the same way they did it the first time.

The Bible clearly teaches us that if we'll repent and learn from our mistakes, our future can be radically changed. That means we have to break free from the old patterns and avoid the same pitfalls the second time around.

Following After Your Own Way

My life has been touched by the story of Jonah. He was a man who made a huge mistake, but when he learned from it, all of the people in a city gave their hearts to the Lord. (Jonah 1-4.)

If you recall the background of this story, there was a large and wealthy, but wicked city called Nineveh. The Bible says that God searched for a man who had a voice, one who was called and anointed to preach repentance to the thousands of citizens, and found such a man in Jonah. He spoke to him, saying, "Go to Nineveh and preach the Gospel for forty days. Their wickedness comes up before Me, and it smells to high heaven. Tell them they're going to be destroyed if they don't repent."

This wasn't a very friendly message. It wasn't the kind of word that sends goose bumps up and down your spine. But the Lord told Jonah to preach it. The voice of God was very clear, and no doubt Jonah felt the awesome presence of the Lord. He knew exactly what God wanted him to do.

However, instead of heading straight for Nineveh, Jonah traveled to the little seacoast town of Joppa, where he booked passage on a boat sailing across the Mediterranean Sea to Tarshish, 180 degrees in the opposite direction from Nineveh. That ship was taking Jonah away from the Lord's calling.

There are many vehicles in this world that take people away from God. Drugs, apathy, and greed are only a few things taking people away from the Savior. No matter who or what is leading you astray, you'd better get off the vehicle that's taking you down the wrong path.

Why Jonah Ran

As I've studied this story over the years, I've often asked myself, "Why did Jonah run from the Lord? Why do men and women run from the call of God on their lives?"

First of all, I believe Jonah ran because he was struggling with racial prejudice. Jonah was a Jew, and Nineveh was a city filled with Gentiles. Jonah didn't want to go to Nineveh because the people were different from him. The world today is steeped in prejudice. People turn their backs on their fellowmen because of the color of their skin or their ethnic background.

So one reason Jonah ran was that he did not want to preach the Gospel to a city of Gentiles. There are many people today who have prejudice in their hearts, and they're not doing what God has called them to do because they don't want to be aligned with a particular group or faction.

Every time I preach in one of the great African-American churches in this country, it's so easy for someone to say, "What is that white guy doing up there ministering to a black congregation?" The answer is very simple. I go where God tells me to go.

I believe the second reason Jonah ran was that he was more concerned about his reputation than he was about the call of God. He was terrified of what someone might think of him if he went to Nineveh. He didn't want to be considered a fool. Why would anybody want to stand on the street corners of that wicked city and shout out loud, "Forty days from now Nineveh will be destroyed. If you don't repent, God is going to wipe you off the face of the earth"?

Jonah didn't want to appear foolish. The apostle Paul declared in 1 Corinthians 4:10 that he was a fool for Christ. He said, "I am not ashamed of the gospel of Christ, for it is the power of God to salvation for everyone who believes" (Rom. 1:16). I am not ashamed to be called a fool for Christ. In fact, 1 Corinthians 1:27 tells us that God takes the things that the world calls foolish and uses them to confound the wise.

I believe the third reason Jonah ran from God's calling is that he thought the Lord would draft somebody else to do the job. A lot of people today have the mistaken idea that if they'll just bide their time long enough, if they'll hide from the limelight a little bit longer, God will get somebody else to do what He has called them to do.

I've got news for you. God didn't spin a globe and point His finger at your hometown and say, "I believe I'll send this person over here." No, it's no accident that you're alive in this hour. You were born for such a time as this. And besides, there's no place where you can hide from the call of God on your life.

You Can't Run From God

That brings me to the fourth reason why I believe Jonah tried to run from the Lord. He actually thought that he could run away from the Almighty. Where can you run to that God isn't there? What airplane can you board, what island can you sail to, what train or boat can you book passage on, or what corner of the earth can you travel to where God isn't present? It's impossible to run away from God's presence. (Ps. 139:7-10.)

Jonah thought he could run from the Lord, but he didn't reckon with the One whose hands scooped out the beds for the oceans, flung the stars from His fingertips, and hung this world on nothing. He didn't reckon with the mighty hand of God.

As soon as the ship got under way, Jonah went down into the bottom of the boat, curled up with his pillow, and fell asleep. In a moment's time, God stretched out His arms and began to breathe over the face of the deep, and the sea began to rustle.

The Lord of the universe began to blow upon those waters until a violent storm erupted. The boat began to pop and crack in the wind as the sails started to rip from their masts. The tempest was so fierce that the ship began to lurch and rock and roll in the crashing waves. The sailors were wild with fear, and they began to cry out to their pagan gods for help. Finally, the captain went below and awakened Jonah, demanding, "How can you sleep at a time like this? Get up and pray to your God, and see if He'll have mercy and save us."

In desperation, the crew decided to cast lots to find out who was causing the storm. When the lot fell on Jonah, he admitted, "I'm the one. I'm running away from the Lord. Throw me overboard, and the sea will become calm. This storm is because of me." Those men didn't have to hear Jonah's words a second time. They picked him up and hurled him into the sea, and the storm stopped.

When Jonah split the waves, the Bible says that God had prepared "a great fish" especially for him, and it gulped him down whole. (Jonah 1:17.) The Bible doesn't say a whale swallowed Jonah. I don't know what kind of fish it was, but it was tailor-made for him by God. The fish had a body that not only accommodated the entire length of Jonah's body but also kept him alive for three days and three nights. Now that's some fish. Really, Jonah was the first man who ever stayed three nights in a floating hotel. He was the first guy who ever rode in a submarine!

If you're on your way to Tarshish today, running from God, I want you to know that God has a special place prepared for you to get back into a right relationship with Him. It may be in the arms of your husband. It may be in the arms of your wife, your parents, or someone else in your family. It may be in the arms of your church or your prayer closet. God has a special place prepared just for you. When you get into that place, you're going to learn from your mistakes, and God is going to show you how to avoid the pitfalls the second time around.

Obedience Brings Victory

In the flash of a second, Jonah found himself trapped inside the belly of that great fish, and he began to cry out to the Lord in his anguish and despair. It's not much fun having seaweed wrapped around your neck and little tiny fish sloshing around your toes.

I can imagine Jonah wading through the deepest, darkest recesses of that fish's belly, calling on God's mercy and crying out to the Lord, "If You'll only get me out of this mess, I'll obey You. Heavenly Father, I promise I'll learn from this mistake." This is what God wanted all along—someone who would walk in obedience to Him.

The instant Jonah declared, "God, I'll do whatever You tell me to do," the fish turned around, swam straight toward the shoreline, and spat Jonah up on the sandy shores. When his feet touched the dry ground, Jonah didn't board another ship headed for Tarshish. No, he set out for Nineveh. He marched straight into the middle of town to obey God and preach the message the Lord gave him.

What a sight Jonah must have been, with his long robe flowing in the breeze and his hair and beard dripping wet and matted with seaweed. He pitched his tent on the most prominent street in town—not on Second Street or Third Street, but on First Street—the main street of the city, the place where the Nineveh National Bank stood. Then he began to shout, "Nineveh, you've got forty days to repent. That's all the time God is going to give you." Jonah stood there in the boiling sun and preached his heart out.

I can picture him with his hands raised in the air, crying out, "If you don't repent, God is going to wipe you off the face of the earth." The people were so jolted by Jonah's message that they believed him and fell on their knees and repented before the Lord. Even the king repented in sackcloth and ashes.

Nineveh was going to hell in a handbasket, but when Jonah obeyed the Lord, much to his shock and amazement, God allowed the citizens of that city to live. In His great mercy, love, and amazing grace, thousands of people whose lives were hanging in the balance repented from their evil ways and were spared from destruction.

God Forgives and Forgets

I've stumbled and made many mistakes in my lifetime. I remember one time when my father asked me, "Richard, you've made a mistake, haven't you?"

"Yes, sir, I have," I replied.

Then he reassured me, "If you'll give your mistake to God by repenting and telling Him that you're sorry for it with all of your heart, I'll stand with you 100 percent."

I was a young man at the time and that absolutely floored me. I asked, "You mean it's that simple?"

I'll never forget my father's answer. He smiled and exclaimed, "Yes, it is."

That's wonderful advice to you today. Many times our mistakes dog our tracks day and night. They hang over us like a cloud, haunting our every waking moment. We serve a God we can run to when we slip and stumble and make mistakes. Psalm 40:2 tells us that the God we serve can handle the miry clay of sin. He can lift us out of the deepest pit, set our feet upon the Rock of our salvation, and establish us.

Perhaps you've been running from the Lord like Jonah was. Or maybe you've been burdened down by a past mistake or sin. Whatever mistakes you may have made, when you repent, God removes your sins from you "...as far as the east is from the west" (Ps. 103:12). In Hebrews 8:12 God says, "I will be merciful...and their sins and their lawless deeds I will remember no more." By the mighty power of the Lord, you can become new—never to be a Jonah man or woman again, but to be a Jesus man, a Jesus woman. Don't carry that old baggage of guilt and shame any longer. Cast your mistakes and burdens onto the Lord and open up your heart to Him.

Look at the life of Jesus as He preached and taught God's Word and healed the people. See how He lived, and try to follow in His footsteps. Be sure to get involved in a strong, Bible-believing, Holy Spirit active church—a church where the minister is on fire for God. The Bible says in Matthew 16:18 that "...the gates of hell shall not prevail against [the church]" (KJV).

Chapter 19

Seventy Times Seven

How do you forgive someone when it seems as if they're pounding you over the head with a lead pipe? How do you forgive somebody when they're spreading terrible lies about you and saying all manner of evil against you? And how can you keep on forgiving them when they keep doing the same things to you over and over again?

The apostle Peter must have been in a situation like that because he asked the Lord, "Jesus, how many times must I forgive someone—seven times?" (Matt. 18:21.) Perhaps Peter had gotten into a squabble with one of his fishing buddies and had already forgiven him seven times. But it had come down to the eighth time, and now Peter's patience was wearing thin. He was really hoping that Jesus would tell him, "Yes, Peter, you only have to forgive seven times," and then he could take his buddy's head off.

Peter had probably given some pretty good spiritual lip service to forgiving that person, but his forgiveness was only skin deep. His heart was full of anger and resentment, and he was just waiting for Jesus to give him the okay so he could knock his friend out with a one-two punch.

I can picture him saying, "Jesus, I hope You realize how many times I've already forgiven this person." The Lord upset Peter's applecart when He replied, "No, Peter, I'm not asking you to forgive seven times, *but seventy times seven*." If you multiply those numbers, Jesus is actually saying that we have to forgive someone 490 times.

If a person needs to be forgiven 490 times, he's probably a real rascal. Yet, the Lord was laying out the Bible principle of forgiveness. He was saying that forgiveness is a continual cycle, a never-ending process. No doubt Peter protested, "But, Lord, You don't know what he's done to me." And perhaps Jesus answered, "It doesn't make any difference, Peter. You have to remain in a continual state of forgiveness."

I can imagine the chief apostle crying out in exasperation, "Well, God, You can forgive him. I don't want to forgive him anymore." But that doesn't work either.

Forgiving When It Hurts

How often are we Christians guilty of offering our prayers to the Lord when our hearts are consumed with unforgiveness? We love to quote the Scripture in Mark 11:24, which says, "Whatever things you ask when you pray, believe that you receive them, and you will have them." Most people don't want to talk about the next verse. In fact, they try to slide right past it. In Mark 11:25 Jesus Christ tells us, "And whenever you stand praying, if you have anything against anyone, forgive him, that your Father in heaven may also forgive you your trespasses."

The bottom line is, if you don't forgive, God will not forgive you. That may sound harsh, but it's the truth. And the Bible says, "You shall know the truth, and the truth shall make you free" (John 8:32).

Now you may be wondering, *Richard, how can I ask for forgiveness and make something right when I'm not the one who caused the problem?* I understand exactly what you're talking about, because I've experienced that very thing myself. Several years ago I was invited to be a guest on a certain national television program, and when I arrived at the studio, I learned that another man was also scheduled to be a guest that same day. Now that particular man had said some pretty cruel things about me on television. I had been deeply offended by his comments, and I was especially upset because what he had said was not true.

Really, I was eaten up with unforgiveness toward that man, and I was upset that God would allow him to appear as a guest with me on the same TV program. I was standing over in a far corner of the room that day, sulking and feeling very sorry for myself. In anger I muttered to the Lord, "Why did You let this man be here today anyway?" You might as well let it all out to God. He already knows what you're thinking anyway.

While I was griping, moaning, and complaining to the Lord, I casually glanced over in that man's direction. When I saw a big smile on his face and the way he seemed to be enjoying himself, I was even more angry. There he was, seemingly having the time of his life, laughing and talking with the people who were crowded all around him, while I was huddled over in the corner by myself, pouting. I was totally miserable because my heart was filled with unforgiveness.

In the flash of a second, God spoke in my spirit and said to me, *Go over there and ask that man to forgive you.*

"What do You mean, Lord?" I quickly protested. "I didn't do anything wrong. I wasn't the one who got up on national television and said something that wasn't true. Why, I haven't even struck back at him. I've been a good, holy Christian."

Then the Holy Spirit urged me again, *Go over there and ask him to forgive you.*

"God, I didn't do anything wrong," I complained bitterly. "I didn't say those cruel things on television. He's the one who owes me an apology."

But the Lord insisted, *You need to ask him to forgive you.*

I waited a few more minutes, and then I swallowed hard. I propped myself up on my right foot for a while, and then I shifted to my left foot, stalling for time.

Finally I muttered, "Okay, Lord," and I marched straight over to that man and stood face to face with him and called him by name. When his eyes met mine, he smiled a great big smile at me and that irked me even more. Nevertheless, I blurted out the words, "I want to ask you to forgive me. I've been holding something against you. I've been wrong, and I'm sorry."

I was shocked when I saw tears well up in his eyes. "Richard," he began, "not long ago I said some things about you that I have discovered are untrue. I have repented before the Lord, and now I ask you to forgive me." Pretty soon I was crying too, and then we threw our arms around each other. A holy forgiveness took place in that room that day. That was one of the hardest things I have ever done, but that man and I have a great relationship in the Lord today. It could never have happened if God hadn't helped me get rid of the unforgiveness in my heart.

If you're harboring unforgiveness against anyone for *any* reason, you need to pluck it out as if it were a deadly cancer because, spiritually speaking, it is a cancer. It will eat you up on the inside. It will turn you sour on the things of God and flood your soul with hatred and bitterness. Eventually it will wreck your life.

When there has been an offense between me and anyone else, even if the other person won't allow me to make it right with him, I tell the Lord, "By faith I choose to forgive that person, and I give him to You. Now he's Your problem, and I don't have to worry about him anymore."

You may say, "But, Richard, you don't know what this person has done to me." No, I don't. But God does. Anyway, it doesn't matter what he has done, because you have to forgive him and give him to the Lord, or God will not forgive you. (Matt. 6:15.) Besides, can you think of a better place for him to be than in God's hands?

No Unforgiveness Here

There is a particular story in the Bible that God has used to bless me concerning forgiveness, and it's the story of Joseph in Genesis 37-47. We've already looked at the story of Joseph, but one thing that's important to remember is that Joseph was a man who freely forgave those who had wronged him—and his forgiveness brought an explosion of miracles into his life.

I'm sure you recall how Joseph was a seventeen-year-old dreamer, the favorite son among the twelve sons of his father, Jacob. His father loved the boy more than all of his other children because he was born to him in his old age. Jacob even had a magnificent handwoven coat of many colors made for him, and when his brothers found out about it they were furious.

Genesis 37:2 says that Joseph also brought bad reports to his father about what his brothers were doing. That suggests he was a tattletale. But he really pushed his brothers over the edge when he began to have big dreams about his future.

Joseph dreamed that he and his brothers were binding sheaves in the field, and his sheaf stood up while their sheaves bowed down to his. He couldn't wait to tell them about his dream, but they bristled because of his cocky attitude. They hated him.

Later he dreamed that the sun, moon, and eleven stars (representing his father, mother, and eleven brothers) bowed down before him. Joseph made the mistake of telling his brothers that dream, too, and they nearly came unglued. His father even rebuked him for it. The Bible says that Jacob pondered the dream in his heart. (Gen. 37:11.)

One day Joseph's brothers herded their flocks to Shechem to graze, and Jacob sent Joseph to check on them. When he arrived in Shechem, there was no sign of his brothers or their flocks, but a man from the area told him they had gone to Dothan. He went after his brothers and found them.

Perhaps the nightlife in Dothan was better than the nightlife in Shechem. Maybe the girls were prettier or the restaurants more appetizing. I can imagine how Joseph's wheels were turning as he rehearsed the story he was going to tell his father.

When his brothers saw him coming that day, they groaned in disgust, "Here comes that dreamer.... Come on, let's kill him.... Then we'll see what will become of all his dreams" (vv. 19,20 TLB). Reuben, his oldest brother, finally convinced them to throw Joseph into a pit instead of killing him—and he planned to come back later and rescue the boy.

They stripped Joseph of his brightly colored coat and shoved him down a well. While they were eating dinner around their campfire, a caravan of Ishmaelite traders rode past them in a cloud of dust. Somehow Judah got the bright idea, "Why don't we sell Joseph to the Ishmaelites? Let's not kill him and have his blood on our hands. After all, he is our brother." And the brothers agreed. What a wonderful way to get rid of their thorn in the flesh—or so they thought.

Joseph was sold into slavery by his very own brothers for the price of twenty pieces of silver. They took his prized coat and smeared it with the blood of a goat and told their father that a wild beast had torn Joseph to pieces. The Bible says that Jacob refused to be comforted, and he mourned bitterly for his son.

Don't Give Up, God Will Bring You Through

Despite all the hurts and misfortunes that befell Joseph, God never left him, and He caused Joseph to prosper as a slave in Egypt. That tells me that God can cause you to prosper wherever you are. You may not be where you ought to be, but thank God, you're not where you used to be. The end of the story hasn't been written yet. You haven't seen the last tomorrow. I believe God will make a way for you if you'll hold true to your God-given vision.

Throughout Joseph's captivity in Egypt, he clung to his God-given dream. When Joseph began to forgive his brothers, God began to restore his life, because forgiveness and restoration go hand in hand. Joseph rose to prominence in the house of a man named Potiphar, a member of the staff of Pharaoh, the king of Egypt. God caused Joseph to shine like a bright star in the land of Egypt. Potiphar was so amazed at the way God's hand was upon this young Hebrew that he turned the management of his own household and all of his lands over to Joseph. Genesis 39:5 says that God blessed the house of the Egyptian because of Joseph.

Naturally, the devil had a hissy fit when he saw how well Joseph was doing, so he decided to set a trap for him. The Bible says that Joseph was a handsome, well-built young man, and Potiphar's wife began to flirt with him. (vv. 6,7.) He always refused her advances, but that only ruffled her pride and made her mad. Day after day she tried every trick she could think of to seduce Joseph, but he always turned her down cold.

One day when they were alone in the house, she pleaded with him once again to go to bed with her, and once again he refused. This time he actually fled from her presence, but as he did, she managed to grab his jacket. When Potiphar returned home that day, his wife greeted him with a wild story she had concocted: "Your Hebrew slave tried to rape me, but when I screamed, he ran." Then she flashed Joseph's jacket in front of Potiphar's eyes, and he became so furious that he had Joseph cast into prison.

At that point many people would have become bogged down with bitterness. Joseph didn't allow those hurts to lodge in his heart. He refused to harbor unforgiveness or wallow in self-pity. Instead, he kept his heart pure. He chose to walk in a spirit of forgiveness, and he rose above the pain and hurt.

It's amazing to see how God's hand was still upon Joseph even after he was thrown into jail. In a very short time, the warden had handed over the administration of the entire prison to Joseph. In fact, all the prisoners reported to him personally.

You may feel as though all hope is gone because the devil has cast you into a deep, dark pit. I declare to you from the Word of God that if you will forgive those who have hurt you and will trust in the Lord, you can expect Him to shine His light down into that pit and cause you to prosper in the middle of your pain and loss. You can expect Him to turn that pit into a fruitful land.

Don't Wallow in Your Trials

In prison, Joseph had every reason to let his past consume him. He could have dwelled on his pain and nursed his hurts. He could have told his sad story to all the other prisoners. Instead, he kept his spirit pure and refused to cling to bitterness or unforgiveness. As a result, God was able to turn around for Joseph's good what the devil meant for evil.

Where did his attitude of forgiveness get him?

One day two prominent men wound up in jail with Joseph. (Gen. 40.) One was the king's chief butler and the other was the king's baker. Joseph was given charge over both of these men. One night each of them dreamed an unusual dream. When they awakened from their sleep, they were extremely troubled, so Joseph asked them what was bothering them. When he learned that they were troubled by dreams, he replied, "Interpreting dreams is God's business. Tell me what you saw" (Gen. 40:8 TLB).

Joseph's gift of interpreting dreams began to change his destiny again. I believe God has given you certain gifts and talents too. If you will be faithful and develop those gifts, they can take you to places you never even dreamed of.

The two men then began to tell their dreams. First, the butler told him, "I dreamed about a vine, and three branches came from the vine, filled with luscious, ripe grapes."

When God gave Joseph the interpretation, he told the man, "The three branches mean that in three days Pharaoh will release you from prison, and the grapes mean that you'll squeeze out the juice and take the cup to Pharaoh once again as his chief butler." Joseph pleaded with him, "When you're restored to the king's favor, please remember me."

The baker's face lit up when he heard that interpretation, and he immediately began to describe his dream to Joseph. "I dreamed there were three white baskets on my head. In the top basket were all kinds of pastries for Pharaoh's table. Before I could present them to the king, a flock of birds swooped down and plucked them out of my basket."

Joseph's face must have turned pale as he looked at the baker in horror. "Sir," he exclaimed, "within three days Pharaoh is going to have you executed, and the birds are going to devour your flesh."

Sure enough, three days later the butler was restored to his place of honor with Pharaoh, and the baker was beheaded and his body hanged, just as Joseph had prophesied. Naturally Joseph must have thought, *Great, now I'm going to get out of here.* But it didn't happen that way. As soon as the butler was released from prison, he promptly forgot about Joseph. The young Hebrew was stranded in a cold, dark jail cell for two more years.

He could have cried out, "Look what I did for that butler, and he forgot all about me!" He could have wallowed in self-pity and blamed others for his troubles. Instead, he chose to overcome those obstacles rather than wallow in them. Joseph chose to sow seeds of forgiveness. It wasn't long until those seeds began to sprout.

One day Pharaoh had a dream, and his magicians, counselors, and so-called wise men couldn't give him the interpretation. Then the chief butler remembered Joseph and said to Pharaoh, "There's a man in prison who can interpret dreams." The king quickly sent for Joseph.

Pharaoh launched into a description of the strange dream which had plagued his sleep. He said, "I was on the bank of a river, and I saw seven fat, healthy-looking cows come up out of the water and begin grazing. Then seven skinny, bony cows came after them and devoured them. "Later I dreamed I saw seven full ears of corn, bulging with grain, on one stalk, and out of the same stalk came seven withered, thin ears. Then the thin ears ate up the seven good ears of corn. When I arose, I told the dream to my wise men and my magicians, but no one could explain it to me."

God gave Joseph the interpretation. He told Pharaoh, "Both dreams are the same. The seven fat cows and seven full ears of corn represent seven years of plenty in Egypt. The seven lean, hungry cows and the seven withered ears of corn represent the seven years of famine that will follow."

Then Joseph urged Pharaoh to appoint a wise administrator to gather up the crops during the seven years of plenty so there would be enough food for the years of famine. Pharaoh was so pleased by Joseph's ability to interpret dreams, and also by his extraordinary wisdom, that he appointed him to be his right-hand man—second in command only to Pharaoh.

Forgiveness Brought Restoration

The seven years of plenty were quickly swallowed up by seven years of famine, just as Joseph had predicted. As the famine ravaged Egypt, it also struck the land of Canaan where Joseph's father and brothers lived.

When Jacob realized that they were running out of food, he sent ten of his sons on a mission to Egypt. Now who do you suppose was on duty to distribute the food to them? Joseph. (Gen. 42.)

As Joseph's brethren pled their case before him, it never crossed their minds that this might be the brother they had betrayed so long ago. Finally, Joseph couldn't hold back the tears any longer. The compassion in his heart came rushing out, and he broke down and began to weep with joy and embrace each of them. "I'm Joseph!" he exclaimed. "I'm the one you sold into slavery. You meant it for harm, but God sent me here to preserve our lives." (Gen. 45:3-5.) He told his brothers to go back to Canaan and bring their father and all of their households to Egypt.

He could have really let them have it and made them grovel in his presence. He could have returned evil for evil. He could have yelled at them, "You dirty, rotten scoundrels. I'm the one you threw into the pit, the one you sold into slavery. You've got a lot of nerve coming to me for help."

Joseph planted a seed of forgiveness in the lives of his brothers, and not only was their whole family reconciled, but God blessed the entire nation of Israel through him.

Joseph went through hell because of what his own brothers did to him. Because of his own flesh and blood, the very people who should have loved him and supported him the most, he spent a good portion of his life as a slave. There are many people today who are grappling with pasts that are so awful that it's almost impossible to imagine the ordeals they've endured. Every day Lindsay and I receive letters and phone calls from people who have been tortured and tormented by the very ones who should have loved them and nurtured them, and it breaks our hearts.

Even if you have gone through hell during your childhood, or perhaps from a former spouse or a loved one—the story of Joseph proves that you don't have to hold on to the wrongdoing and lose your hope.

You can forgive those who have hurt you. You can release all that mess to God, and your future can be as bright as the dawn.

Standing in the Gap

Recently the Lord gave my wife, Lindsay, a powerful revelation on the subject of forgiveness, and I want her to share in her own words what God revealed to her:

One day Richard gave me a copy of a book entitled **The Importance of Forgiveness,**[2] *which the author, John Arnott, had sent to him. John Arnott is associated with the Toronto Blessing.*

While I was reading this book, the Lord began to minister to me about His way to release people and bless those who have hurt us. I believe many people today are harboring hurts and bitterness, and they're buried deep down on the inside. If they could ever release those offenses and get that hurt out of their spirit man, then God could freely pour out His healing power on their lives.

The Lord showed me through John Arnott's book that when you bless those who have hurt you, you're not giving them what you think they need, but you're giving them what the Lord knows they need. You're giving them mercy.

When people wrong you, they deserve the judgment of God. You can bless them by standing in the gap between them and their punishment by saying, "Father God, I beg for mercy on their behalf." In other words, you stand in the gap for the person who least deserves it in your sight, and you ask God to give them mercy.

The Lord Jesus Christ was our greatest example of what I'm talking about. When He hung on the cross, He stood in the gap for the people who had beaten Him, the ones who had applied those thirty-nine stripes to His back and crucified Him. He prayed, "Father, forgive them, for they do not know what they do" (Luke 23:34). In other words, He was saying, "God, give them mercy, not judgment."

If you hold judgment and bitterness against others, not only are they sinners—because of what they have done to you—but you become just as much of a sinner as they are when you refuse to forgive them and release them to God.

---

[2] John Arnott, *The Importance of Forgiveness*, (Sovereign World, Ltd, 1997).

That means Satan has the legal right and authority, as the accuser of the brethren, to stand before the Lord and accuse you, saying, "God, they have stood in the seat of judgment. Now You're going to have to judge them too." (Rev. 12:10.) But, if you'll only show mercy, you'll receive mercy from God.

If you think about it, as long as you're alive and breathing, you're going to goof up sometime, somewhere. If you've been judgmental, then God has to multiply judgment back to you. If you decide to stand in the gap for the ones who have hurt you and bless them with mercy and forgiveness, then the Lord will take that precious mercy and multiply it back to you. He won't pour out the punishment or judgment that you deserve, but He'll multiply mercy right back to you.

When Lindsay shared that revelation with me, it shook me to the core of my being. What it all boils down to is this: You haven't really forgiven others until you've stood in the gap for them and prayed that God would be merciful to them. (Luke 6:28.) Now that's the hallmark of true Bible forgiveness.

A Biblical Commandment

It's important for us to live in a constant state of forgiveness. Didn't Jesus tell us in the Lord's Prayer that we should ask God to forgive us our trespasses or wrongdoings as we forgive those who have wronged us? (Matt. 6:12.) That doesn't mean we should be gullible or allow ourselves to be walked on like a doormat. Nor can we harbor unforgiveness.

When people have wounded, wronged, or abused you or your loved ones, sow a seed of forgiveness into their lives. You can then expect God to take His heavenly bucket and pour out the oil of forgiveness on you. Forgiveness isn't just a nice idea. It's a biblical requirement given to us by the Lord.

Chapter 20

Faith Brings the How-To

Before becoming president of Oral Roberts University, I had under-gone extensive training while I served for eight years as executive vice president. When I stepped into the office of president, I believed the anointing would come upon me to operate in that office. In the natural, however, I didn't know how to turn the debt situation of the university around. Eventually, I decided to believe that I could, and the how-to has shown up. There are things God has called you to do, and you've been stuck in your comfort zone, wondering whether or not you'll ever be able to accomplish them. If you'll believe God, the how-to will show up. Didn't Jesus say, "All things are possible to him who believes"? (Mark 9:23). God doesn't call the equipped. He equips the called.

When I first started grappling with the $56 million debt, I felt over-whelmed, totally inadequate, whipped, and beaten down. Many times I was jolted awake in the middle of the night with the strain of that hellish situation ripping me apart. There was no way I could deal with the debt in the natural. I didn't have training in business. My bachelor's degree is in communications, and I've also earned a master's degree and a doctor of ministry degree from the ORU School of Theology and Missions. I've never received any formal training in business.

Over the years I've taken a crash course in business, while at the same time I've been learning how to be a college educator. In addition, I've had to remain true to my calling as an evangelist in the healing ministry. How can a person do all of that? By believing that you can. Then, as you step out in faith, the how-to shows up. If you don't step out, the how-to won't show up.

I take no personal credit for ORU's debt being slashed. I take no personal credit for the tremendous upswing in applications and enrollment. I give God all the glory for those great miracles. I've also been surrounded by a great team of coworkers, and Lindsay has been my helper. Still God couldn't have accomplished those things through me if I hadn't stepped out of my comfort zone and believed that the how-to would show up.

Take the Limits Off

I remember the story of a man in the Bible who had to step out of his comfort zone and believed that the how-to would show up. In Mark 9, Jesus and three of His disciples had descended from the Mount of Transfiguration to find that the other disciples were ministering to a man whose son was tormented by a demon.

When the father took the boy to the disciples, no doubt his heart was supercharged with faith. He must have heard about the remarkable miracles Jesus had performed. Perhaps he had heard about the way the Lord had cast a whole legion of demons out of the man from Gadara. (Mark 5:1-15.) No doubt he thought, *If He can cast out a legion of demons, surely He can take care of one demon that's plaguing my child.* Yet, no matter how hard the disciples prayed, they couldn't break Satan's grip off his son.

He was standing in the presence of nine of the most trusted men on the face of the earth, and they failed miserably. Fear suddenly gripped his heart. At first he was filled with faith, but now his heart is flooded with doubt. He whirled around to see Jesus Christ walking toward him and cried out, "Jesus, nine of Your men couldn't help me. But if *You* can do anything, please help me," as if the Lord of the universe couldn't do anything. (Mark 9:17,18.)

Because of the disciples' inability to cast the demon out of the boy, the man's doubts had been magnified. He said to Jesus, "If *You* can do anything, please help me."

How many times have you and I gone to God in our humanness and exclaimed in exasperation, "O Lord, I've done everything I know to do. If *You* can do anything about this situation, please help me," as if God couldn't do everything.

What was Jesus' response? He first addressed the disciples, saying, "How long am I going to have to put up with your unbelief?" Then He turned to the boy's father and declared, "If *you* can believe, all things are possible to him who believes." (v. 23.) Those are strong words. Jesus was saying, "You can have whatever you can believe for." That is a powerful thought. The man cried out and said with tears, "Lord, I do believe, but I still have this one little pocket of unbelief over here that I don't know how to deal with. Lord, please help me with my unbelief."

And that's the way so many of us are today. Our hearts are filled with faith. Yet, there is still a little twinge of doubt over in one corner of our minds, and it crops up to torment us every now and then. Jesus is telling us that we can take our faith, which is our launching pad for miracles, and believe. The how-to will show up.

The Lord commanded them, "Bring the boy to Me." He rebuked the foul spirit that was plaguing the child, and with a violent cry it wrenched his body as it left him. The boy collapsed in a heap on the ground, and the crowd gasped, thinking he must be dead, but "Jesus took him by the hand and lifted him up, and he arose" (v. 27).

That young man was set free from the stranglehold of the devil, all because his father launched out in faith and waited for the how-to to show up. To receive your miracle, you have to launch out and believe that you can and then expect the how-to to show up.

God's Way Is Different Than Your Way

As I walked through the valley of the "shadow of debt" at ORU, I believed I could deal with it, not in my own strength, but I believed that God would anoint me to deal with it. I believed that if I worked hard, prayed and trusted God, and sowed my seeds, the how-to would show up. I can testify that it has been showing up ever since.

Wherever I go in the city of Tulsa, Oklahoma, business people, who don't even know the Lord but who have witnessed the amazing turn-around at ORU, have walked up to me, patted me on the back, and exclaimed, "Richard, you're doing such a wonderful job." I tell them, "I give all the glory to God."

It's no different in your life. The how-to will show up for you in the same way that it shows up for me. If you're a businessman or a business-woman, if you're in the marketplace or in the ministry, if you're at home with children, or if you're an educator, no matter what the calling of God upon your life is, if you believe you can, the how-to will show up. I'm not talking about somebody who is sitting in their prayer closet, twiddling their thumbs and waiting for miracles to come raining down from heaven. There is a time to work, because James 2:26 declares that faith without works is dead. We've got to work hard and then combine our faith with our works. As we do, the how-to will show up.

God's how-to may come into your life in an entirely different way from the way you thought it would, because His ways are higher than your ways, and His thoughts are higher than your thoughts. (Isa. 55:9.)

If I were the Lord, Richard Roberts would be the last person on earth I would have selected to put at the helm of a major university. I can see my heavenly Father, chuckling to Himself and saying, "I'm going to take the least likely one and use him for My glory." God called me out of my comfort zone to be the president of Oral Roberts University, and I didn't have a clue about how to do it. But I knew that if I believed I could, God would anoint me and He would show me the way. In the same way, no matter what kind of hellish battle you're facing, the Word of God declares: If you believe you can, God's *how-to* will show up.

Chapter 21

How I Became Another Man

What a glorious moment it was when the prophet Samuel anointed Saul to be the first king of Israel—God's choice to be the ruler of His people. Let me set the scene for you as this dramatic story from the Bible unfolds.

First Samuel 10:1 declares, "Then Samuel took a flask of oil and poured it upon his [Saul's] head, and kissed him." This is not referring to a sexual kiss. It's symbolic of the kiss of God coming upon Saul's life. No doubt Samuel laid his hands upon the new king as he said, "The Spirit of the Lord will come upon you, and you will prophesy with them and be turned into another man" (v. 6).

If ever a Scripture was written for my life, it's this Scripture. I had no more earthly idea how to be the president of Oral Roberts University when I was first elected to that office than Saul had of how to be the king of Israel. Samuel prophesied to him, "The Spirit of the Lord will come upon you."

When I stepped into the office of president of ORU, I felt inadequate to fill that position. There was no way for me to grasp what it would be like to be the president and chief executive officer of a world-class university. Until I moved into that position, there was no way I could imagine what it would entail. It would be like trying to imagine what it's like to strap on a parachute and hurl yourself from an airplane. Until you actually strap on that parachute and take a flying leap into the sky, you have no idea what it's like.

Now the Lord told Saul, "The Spirit of the Lord will come upon you," signifying that God would give him a fresh anointing to stand in the office of king. When my father announced that he would step down as president of ORU, I spent many intense hours in prayer, crying out to the Lord for a double portion of His anointing. God began answering my prayer and flooding my life with a powerful new anointing for that office.

Then the Lord declared to Saul through the prophet Samuel, "And you will prophesy…." Remember, the gift of prophecy is one of the nine gifts of the Holy Spirit described in 1 Corinthians 12:8-10, but I don't believe this is merely a word about the gift of prophecy. I believe it's a word about all nine gifts of the Spirit. Samuel was saying, "Not only will the Spirit of the Lord come upon you, but the gifts of the Spirit will burst alive in your life." There's been a mighty explosion of the gifts of the Spirit surging through my life, especially during the past few years.

Not only has the operation of the word of knowledge increased dramatically, but I've also begun to feel the power of the Lord burning and moving through my hands like never before. I feel a holy heat flowing through me as I'm praying for the healing of others, and yet there's no physical sign of redness. There's no fire, but suddenly there is a holy heat burning through my hands. It's as if the Spirit of God is pumping through my hands like a powerful current of fire.

Samuel then told the new king, "You're going to be turned into another man." Since I have become president of Oral Roberts University, I feel as if I've become another man. My wife concurs and has told me, "Richard, you're a different person now." Even though my outward circumstances didn't turn around the instant I received the joy of the Lord, I changed on the inside. The Spirit of God came upon me, the gifts of the Spirit began flowing in a greater measure through my life, and I became another man.

Even though I was still dealing with some of the same nightmarish problems I was facing before, I was filled with a joy that lifted me above the turmoil. I'm talking about a manifestation of holy joy and laughter that takes over your life, and you're not the same anymore. Something new exploded in the life of Richard Roberts. I became a new man because of the joy of the Lord.

Finishing Your Course With Joy

In Acts 20:24, the apostle Paul declared triumphantly, "But none of these things move me." What is he talking about here? None of these trials, these tribulations—none of these experiences of being whipped with rods, stoned with rocks, hurled into prison, and wrapped in cruel chains—none of these things move me! Then he added, "Neither do I esteem my life dear to myself, if only I may finish my course with joy and the ministry which I have obtained from...the Lord Jesus, faithfully to attest the good news (Gospel) of God's grace" (AMP).

That Scripture is the cry of my heart today, and I hope it's the cry of your heart as well. There's a sighing, crying, dying world out there, and they're going to be lost and damned forever unless they are snatched from the jaws of hell. If we're going to pull them out of Satan's grasp, we have to have the joy of the Lord, which is our strength. It's the joy of the Lord that shines through our lives that will draw the lost to Christ.

You may be thinking, *I remember a time when my heart was full of joy, but I don't know how to sustain God's joy in my life.* I'm so glad you mentioned that subject because I've had many opportunities to allow Satan to drive the joy right out of my life. Just because I had a visitation from God in the summer of 1993, turned a Holy Ghost somersault in mid-air, and experienced a mighty river of joy erupting down in my soul doesn't mean that I wake up every morning with a smile plastered across my face. No. I have countless opportunities to lose my joy every day, the same as you do.

There have been many times over the last few years when the devil took a deadly aim at our entire ministry, even as there was an ominous cloud of debt hanging over this place. In other words, I didn't wake up one morning and all of a sudden—*poof*—everything was smooth sailing. I've had to stir up the joy of the Lord in my life exactly as you have to do.

Stirring Up That Which Is Within

How do I stir up the joy of the Lord? How do I keep a joyous expectancy for miracles bubbling up in my soul? First, I stay in an attitude of praise and worship. I'm not going to wait for the rocks to cry out with their praise and worship to the Savior. I'm going to shout my praise to God with a voice of thanksgiving and let my worship ring out until the foundations of heaven begin to shake. Praise and worship are a vital part of sustaining God's joy in my life. The joy of the Lord doesn't just happen.

I have days when my telephone rings early and the devil tries to blot out my joy with some kind of heartrending news. But I've made a determined decision to finish my course with joy. The apostle Paul proclaimed in Philippians 3:14, "I press toward the goal for the prize of the upward call of God in Christ Jesus." Like Paul, I've also made an uncompromising decision to press toward the mark for the prize.

I begin my day by lying before the Lord flat on my face on my living room carpet. I begin to worship the Lord unashamedly from the depths of my soul because He is a God who glories and revels in our praises. I lift my prayer of thanksgiving to Him. I pray over my family. I pray over our ministry and ORU. I put a Holy Ghost prayer cover over them all. I speak to finances and command them to come in. I tell the devil to take his hands off God's property.

When I'm driving to the office, I often pull off the road somewhere on the beautiful grounds of Oral Roberts University and begin to prayerfully meditate on the Word of God. As the leader of ORU and our ministry, I put on the whole armor of God by faith for our corporate body. (Eph. 6:10-18.)

I put on the powerful belt of truth so I can be a soul winner for the Lord Jesus Christ. Then I put on my breastplate of righteousness to protect my heart, with which I believe upon the Savior. Next, I reach down and pull on my gospel shoes so I can trample boldly over the devil's roughest territory. And I also cover my head with the helmet of salvation, bringing my mind into subjection to my spirit.

I take my Bible in my hand, which is the sword of the Spirit, the Word of God. It's a powerful, razor-sharp weapon which I can use to cut the devil down to size. By faith, I hold my shield of faith up high as if I'm fending off the fiery missiles of the evil one—shielding myself, my family, the university, and our ministry against all of his death-dealing blows.

Then I take what I believe is the seventh piece of my mighty, invincible, Holy Ghost armor, and I begin to pray in tongues and also interpret back to my mind by praying in English.

Before I know it, no matter what kind of bad news the devil hurls at me that day, no matter whether it appears that all of my hopes have been dashed to pieces, my face is smiling. The joy of the Lord is bubbling up in my heart and I'm looking the world straight in the eye.

I'm not simply going through empty, meaningless motions as I pray. I'm engaged in high-powered spiritual warfare against the enemy of my soul. This divine, Holy Ghost joy and laughter packs a powerful wallop against the devil.

I'm also saying to the Lord, "Help me stir up the river of joy that's lying dormant in my heart." It's like those old-style pumps we used to have many years ago. You had to pour a little cup of water in the well to prime the pump. You had to put a little water in so you could get a lot of water gushing back out. When I'm praying each morning, I'm really priming my spiritual pump.

I'm doing what Paul described in Acts 26:2 when he declared, "I think myself happy." He made an earnest, wholehearted decision of his faith to think himself happy. In the same regard, there's a Holy Ghost decision-maker on the inside of me, and I've made a decision that I'm not going to lose the joy of the Lord or allow the devil to take it away from me.

There are some mornings when I may need to have a good old-fashioned "attitude adjustment," so I declare by faith, "Lord, I resist this rotten, stinking attitude. I recognize that this is a strategy of Satan, and I refuse to give the devil any place in my life. I'm going to hold my head up, put my shoulders back, and have a heart full of joy and thanksgiving unto the Lord."

Sometimes as I drive across campus, I break out into joy-filled, hilarious laughter right there in my car. If somebody were to drive by and glance over at me, they might think, *Richard, you're crazy. You're out of your mind.* Yes, I am out of my mind, but I'm not crazy. I'm into my spirit, where God created me to be.

Don't misunderstand what I'm saying here. I'm not advocating acting weird or flaky. I'm not parading up and down the streets of downtown Tulsa, Oklahoma, making a spectacle of myself.

But when the Spirit of God moves on me, that's a different story. But I'm not talking about doing something that's strange or irrational. I'm talking about something that's based on the rock-solid foundation of

God's Word. I'm talking about something that's desperately needed if the church is going to shine in this sin-darkened world.

Put on a Bigger Coat

You may be thinking, *Richard, I'm just not a strong Christian. I can't possibly discipline myself that way.* It's time for you to come to grips with the realities of life. It's time to square your shoulders and stand tall, lest you be trampled by the onslaught of Satan that's being unleashed upon this earth.

I remember a very soul-stirring sermon my dad used to preach, entitled, "Put on a Bigger Coat." That means you're going to have to lengthen your tent cords like the Bible says to do in Isaiah 54:2. You're going to have to cast aside those paralyzing fears and enlarge the borders of your tent—enlarge your vision of God's plan and purpose for your life.

It's time to stop protesting. You say, "I'm shy. I'm too intimidated to do something like that." You may be someone who cowers at the very sight of your own shadow, but God's Word proclaims: "God has not given us a spirit of fear, but of power and of love and of a sound mind" (2 Tim. 1:7). It's time for you to become another man or woman and become the person God created you to be.

You may be someone who's sitting in the dark with your arms folded, staring at the ceiling and waiting for God to move. This Christian life is no free ride. There's no hocus-pocus to it. It's real. It takes grit, faith, fortitude, God's grace, and human determination. You've got to stiffen your will and have the courage and backbone to stand up straight and tall for Jesus and do your part.

I'm praying that you'll grab hold of this with your whole heart because I believe the time is short. The Bible says that in the twinkling of an eye we'll be snatched from this earth to be with the Lord forever.

(1 Cor. 15:52.) In the meantime, we've got to be bold-hearted, faith-filled believers in Jesus, raising up a mighty banner for the kingdom of God. We can't lift that blood-stained banner to the sky without a great big double dose of the joy of the Lord.

Riding on the Crest of Holy Ghost Joy

I want you to buckle your seat belt as you read this Scripture because I believe it's going to hit home in your heart.

In your day of trouble, may the Lord be with you! May the God of Jacob keep you from all harm.

May he send you aid from his sanctuary in Zion.

May he remember with pleasure the gifts you have given him, your sacrifices and burnt offerings.

May he grant you your heart's desire and fulfill all your plans.

May there be shouts of joy when we hear the news of your victory, flags flying with praise to God for all that he has done for you. May he answer all your prayers!

PSALM 20:1-5 TLB

When I read this Scripture, it was like a bomb exploded in my spirit. It struck such a strong chord in me that I thought to myself, *That Scripture is for me.* I believe that Scripture is for you, too.

By faith, the day is about to burst on the horizon when ORU's wall of debt will tumble to the ground. When that day comes, there will be shouts of joy and flags streaming in the air. There will be people rejoicing wildly, sending up a roar of praise to almighty God for all the great things He's done for us.

My mind flashes back to the time when ORU received official accreditation and my dad proclaimed a special celebration on the ORU campus. What a celebration it was! I believe we ought to have an old-fashioned, hallelujah, Holy Ghost blowout on the day ORU breaks free from debt. I believe it's not going to be long.

I have a dream that floods my soul—a dream for ORU. In my spirit, I see the debt being totally wiped out. I see the endowment beginning to mushroom, and I see new buildings exploding out of the ground.

I'm serious about the future of Oral Roberts University because there are countless lives hanging in the balance. I have a vision of young people streaming from the doors of ORU to every nation, every tribe, every tongue, every people, spreading the good news of the Gospel throughout every man's world. I see the brightest future that I've ever seen, and I give all the glory to God.

You may be thinking, *Richard, where's your evidence for that?* My faith is the evidence. My faith is bursting out of my chest today because I've caught a glimpse of something on the horizon—for Oral Roberts University and for your life, too. Before God can hurtle those obstacles out of our path, we've got to have a dose of the joy of the Lord.

Why? Because it was holy joy and laughter that opened a pipeline to God's power in my life. It was a happy, hilarious spirit of joy which produced a revolutionary change in me. In just a short time, I was transformed into another man. I have living proof that the joy of the Lord works—and I want to see it working in your life, too.

Every time I'm hanging over the edge of a precipice, every time Satan issues another death threat against ORU, I start laughing in the Spirit and praising Jesus, the Rock of my salvation, and God continues to turn Satan away from our door. I'm free from that horrendous stress level. I'm free from those terrible ulcers that were plaguing me. I'm riding on the crest of God's Holy Ghost joy.

Meanwhile, ORU has been transformed. Our television program has been set on fire by the Spirit of God. Reports are streaming in from people all over the world who are rejoicing, saying, "The joy of the Lord has overtaken my life, and I'm not the same person anymore."

Chapter 22

Turning Your Life Around

Perhaps you are thinking, *I've been struggling for a long time and feel as though all of my hope is gone. I can't seem to get out of the hell I'm in.* Maybe several months or even years have passed since this situation began, and it seems that no matter how hard you struggle to break free, it is still clinging to you like a deadly vise grip.

I remember a moving story in the Bible about a woman whose hope was just about gone because of a hemorrhage that had flowed from her body for twelve long years. (Luke 8:43-48.) I want you to picture this woman slumped on the edge of her bed, weeping, feeling cut off from the world. She was desperate, bewildered, and at the end of her way. Not only was the very life being drained out of her through this terrible flow of blood, but she also was ostracized and shunned by the people around her because of her condition. You see, in those days anyone who had an issue of blood was considered to be unclean.

You may be suffering from something that has cut you off from the rest of the world. Perhaps it's a crippling disease or paralysis, or maybe it's some type of pain that has wracked your body and kept you from living a normal, active life.

Not only did this woman suffer isolation, but the Bible says that she suffered many things from many physicians—perhaps extensive medical tests and procedures. In fact, she had spent virtually all of her money searching for a cure, but her condition had only deteriorated. No doubt the doctors had genuinely tried to help her, but medicine was of such a primitive nature in those days that there was very little they could do for her.

You may be at the very same point this woman was. You may have suffered many things from many physicians. Although they've tried desperately to help you, the medical procedures were so grueling, so invasive, and had such horrible side effects, that you've suffered almost more from the treatment than you've suffered from the disease.

To top things off, instead of getting better, you've lost ground. Your condition has taken a nosedive, and now you're at your wits' end. That's exactly where this woman found herself. Then something happened that dramatically changed her life. She heard about Jesus. *The Amplified Bible* says, "She had heard the reports concerning Jesus" (Mark 5:27). *The Living Bible* says, "She heard all about the wonderful miracles Jesus did."

There probably isn't a person alive in the United States today who hasn't heard something about Jesus. But did you know that you can go to church all of your life and hear about Jesus with your physical ears and still never hear about the real Jesus with your spiritual ears? Somehow it may not have registered in your spirit who Jesus really is. You haven't grasped that His is the only power that can wash away your sins, heal every disease that's invaded your body, and deliver you from whatever is troubling your soul.

When the woman with the issue of blood heard about Jesus, it dawned on her that it was the Lord's very nature to heal. She immediately got excited about it and began to declare out loud, "If I can only touch the hem of His garment, I shall be made whole." *The Amplified Bible* says that she kept repeating the words over and over again: "If I only touch His garment, I shall be restored to health" (Matt. 9:21).

Facing the Impossible

If you've ever faced a life-and-death battle of your faith, if you've ever taken your stand on God's Word and declared the Scriptures out loud day and night, then you understand what this woman was doing. She was fighting for her existence with the words of her mouth. Proverbs 18:21 tells us, "Death and life are in the power of the tongue."

When you're believing God for a healing and you're proclaiming the healing Scriptures by faith over your body, then you can expect those Scriptures to go off in your spirit like a mighty rocket. Your faith will connect with God in a way that it has never connected before, and it will suddenly dawn on you that God's Word is true.

You will know it deep in your soul, and nothing will be able to shake you from it—no heartbreaking reports from the doctor, no symptoms raging in your body, no negative words spoken over you. You will know that you know that you know that God's Word is true.

You may be thinking, *But, Richard, I've been saying the Scriptures and saying the Scriptures, and I'm still in the same condition I was in before I started saying them.* Just keep proclaiming God's Word in faith. He said in Isaiah 55:11, "My Word...shall not return to Me void, but it shall accomplish what I please, and it shall prosper in the thing for which I sent it." What did God send His Word to do? Psalm 107:20 declares that "He sent His Word and...delivered them from their destructions."

God's Word will *not* return void. As long as you obey His Word, speak His Word, and do the things that He has spoken in your heart to do, you can expect His Word to accomplish what He sent it to do in your life. You say, "But I've suffered so long." The woman with the issue of blood had suffered for many years, but she still received her deliverance. God's Word accomplished what He sent it to do in her life.

Let me ask you an important question. What did this woman do to get her deliverance? First, she did what she felt the Holy Spirit was prompting her to do. Likewise, you must do what you feel God speaking in your heart to do. It's important to follow the leading of God's Spirit.

This woman's miracle started when she began to say what God said about her situation, and she kept on speaking a word of healing over her life until she was healed. Saying the Word is such a powerful force for your deliverance. No matter how strongly you believe God's Word, it doesn't become Holy Ghost dynamite that can blast away your mountain of problems until you speak it with your mouth.

Many people have rejected the teaching that you should confess your faith through the words you speak, but the very basis of the Christian faith is the confession of Jesus Christ as Lord and Savior. Romans 10:9-10 declares, "If you confess with your mouth the Lord Jesus and believe in your heart that God has raised Him from the dead, you will be saved. For with the heart one believes unto righteousness, and with the mouth confession is made unto salvation." I tell you, it's absolutely vital for you to speak God's words continually, and then watch His Holy Ghost dynamite blast the mountains of obstacles out of your way.

In Luke's gospel the Bible gives us another important clue about why this woman received her healing from the Lord. Luke 8:47 says "...she declared to Him in the presence of all the people the reason [or for what purpose] she had touched Him and how she was healed immediately."

You've got to have a sense of purpose about you when you go to God. You can't simply think, *Well, I'll drift along and somehow, some way, God will do for me what I need done.* It doesn't work that way. You've got to focus your faith on what you want from the Lord. I don't mean tomorrow; I mean *today*.

Pressing Through the Obstacles

You may be thinking, *You don't know all the obstacles I'm facing. I've wrestled so hard to get a breakthrough, but I seem to be at a standstill.* This woman faced more obstacles than most of us have ever faced, but she refused to back down on her faith.

Let's think about her situation for a moment. Her condition had dragged on for twelve long years. She was probably skin and bones. A stream of blood was hemorrhaging from her body. No doubt she felt lightheaded, perhaps on the verge of passing out. Yet, somehow she managed to get up that morning, get dressed, and go out and fight her way through the crowd that surrounded Jesus. Why, she wasn't even supposed to come in contact with other people. After all, she was considered unclean. And, besides, how could she possibly get through to Jesus? *The Message Bible* says that Jesus was "making his way through the pushing, jostling crowd" (Luke 8:42).

In my imagination I can see this woman crouching down and crawling through the mass of people surrounding Jesus, brushing them aside in a gentle but strong way. "Please excuse me!" she exclaimed. "I've got to get to the Master. I've had this issue of blood for twelve years. I've spent all of my money trying to get well, but I'm growing weaker. Sir, please excuse me. Ma'am, won't you let me through." Suddenly she saw the Lord standing before her. She could see His sandals, His robe, and His prayer shawl wrapped around His body—the garment she had been straining with all of her might to touch. It's important for you to realize that Jesus' prayer shawl was the same type of garment that was worn by the rabbis in that day, and its tassels represented the Word of God.

This woman was hungry for God's Word. She knew that her deliverance was in the Word. She had been speaking God's Word, confessing it with her mouth, and believing it in her heart. As a point of contact to release her faith, she was ready to reach out and touch the Word of God.

In the next split second, she grabbed the border of Jesus' garment. It was as if she were standing in a pool of water and somebody flipped a switch and turned on the electricity. The power of God surged through her body, and the Bible says that Jesus whirled around and exclaimed, "Who touched Me?"

No doubt the disciples glared at Him in dismay. I can picture Peter shrugging his shoulders as he blurted out, "Give us a break, Jesus. Everybody is brushing up against You. Everybody is crying out, 'Jesus, touch me. Jesus, heal me. Jesus, cleanse me.' And now You want to know who touched You. Come on, Lord. We don't have any idea who touched You."

Think about all the commotion that was going on around the Master that day. This woman had to press through some major roadblocks to receive her deliverance. When she saw all the people, she didn't throw up her hands and exclaim, "Oh, the crowd is too big. There's no way I can get to Jesus." She didn't declare, "There's no way I can get a seat on the front row of that healing service, so I'm not going to go."

If you need a miracle from God, you'd better do something about it. Get down on your knees; fall on your face before the Lord. Do whatever it takes to get yourself into the presence of the Lord. You may be able to meet with God right there in your own living room, or you may need to go to a healing crusade. I don't know what you need to do, but the Lord knows. Be quick to obey what He speaks in your heart.

She Was Healed and Made Whole

When the woman with the issue of blood touched Jesus' garment, He felt something and she felt something. (Luke 8:46,47.) Many people get so hung up on the fact that faith is not a feeling (which is true), they forget that many times you can feel the power of God moving in your life.

You don't have to feel anything in order to be healed, but this woman felt her faith moving, and Jesus felt her faith draw the healing power out of His body. That's why He asked His disciples, "Who touched Me?" He felt the power rush out of Him. The Scripture also says that she felt in her body that she was healed. And no doubt she physically felt the flow of blood dry up.

According to 2 Corinthians 5:7, we walk by faith and not by sight, and we certainly don't walk by our feelings. If you can feel strawberry ice cream sliding down your throat, then you can feel faith. You can feel the presence of the Lord. You can feel His power rushing through your body. You can experience a "feeling of healing." We don't walk by that feeling of healing, but it can be a powerful boost to our faith. It can help us keep pressing on until we receive the manifestation of our miracle.

Her Faith Made Her Whole

Whether the woman with the issue of blood ever felt anything in her body or not, as soon as she touched the hem of Jesus' garment—her point of contact—it was time for her to start thanking God for her healing. It was time for her to rejoice in her soul because Jesus' word to her said that she *was* healed.

Think about what an experience this must have been for this woman. When she awakened that morning, she was terribly weak from the condition which had battered her body for so many years. She was probably beaten down in her spirit because she had been an outcast for so long. She'd been told there was no hope for her. Medical science had given her up to die. She was at the bottom of the heap when she touched Jesus' garment. All of a sudden, everything changed. When the Master asked, "Who touched Me," she confessed what had happened in her body. She was bold in her faith, and Jesus rewarded her faith with an extraordinary miracle.

I want you to listen to what Jesus said to her next. He called her *daughter.* I know what a daughter means to her daddy, for I surely know what my daughters mean to me. In that one word, the love of Jesus flooded through every fiber of her being. *Daughter,* He called her. Then He said, "Your faith has made you well." Notice He did *not* say, "My overwhelming power has made you well," yet His power certainly *was* overwhelming. He didn't say, "My high-powered preaching has made you well." He didn't say, "The compassion of My Father has made you well." He didn't say, "Somebody else's faith has made you well." He said, "Daughter, your faith has made you well."

If her faith made her whole, then your faith can make you whole, too, because God is no respecter of persons. Romans 12:3 declares that God has given to every person *the* measure of faith. Now that you know you have it, it's time to use it.

I believe you need to hear the Lord saying to you right now, "My son, my daughter." You need to hear it deep within your soul. You need to hear Him saying to you, "Your faith is healing your body. Your faith is blasting away that thing that has been troubling you, which you feel can't get any worse." Through your faith, you can cast that problem out. Reach out and grab hold of the hem of Jesus' garment. Begin to call your healing down from the Lord. If you stand on the Word of God, you can expect God to hurl Satan out of your way.

Chapter 23

The End of an Uphill Climb

When you're running a race, the last stretch is always the most challenging. It's hard to describe the feeling that sweeps over you when you round that last turn and see the finish line looming in the distance before you. Many a great horse has seemingly run out of leg power by the time it entered the home stretch. But then something in the horse's spirit took over, and it began to run with heart. That's what I've been doing in the midst of the battles I've fought at ORU. I've been running with heart.

When the hosts of hell are blasting you and Satan's bombs and mortars are exploding around you, there are times when you feel as if your legs can't hold you up any longer. That's when your heart has to take over. However, if it hasn't dawned on you that you're coming to the end of an uphill climb, it's not easy for your heart to take over.

Probably one of the best illustrations of this is found in Luke 5:17-26 of a man who had been paralyzed for a long time, his limbs completely lifeless. He had four friends who cared enough to lift him up, and they took him to the top of an uphill climb. I thank God for someone who will pick you up when you're knocked down, when you're strapped financially, when you're gripped by a spirit of loneliness, when it feels as if the props have been knocked out from under you.

That's what these four men did. They lifted up their friend who was paralyzed, struck down by a terrible, crippling paralysis, and they declared, "We're going to take you to Jesus." I can picture them in my mind's eye, hurrying through the busy streets of the city, carrying their friend on a stretcher, and telling him miracle stories about Jesus.

They must have said, "Did you hear about the man who was blind, and Jesus spat on the ground and made a mudpack out of the spittle, then smeared it on the man's eyes, and he was healed?" (John 9:1-7.) Or they must have said to him, "Did you hear about how the Lord raised Jairus's daughter from her deathbed?" (Luke 8:49-56.) Or, "Did you hear about the way Jesus multiplied a few loaves and fishes and fed fifteen thousand people?" (Matt. 14:15-21.) I know if I had been carrying my friend to Jesus, I would have been filling him full of faith-building, miraculous testimonies.

When the men arrived at the house where the Lord was preaching, there was such a huge crowd that they couldn't get through the door. There was seemingly no way for them to get to the Master.

This is where a lot of people are today. They have run head-on into a major obstacle, and they are just sitting there, staring at it, while the miracle they're believing for could be just beyond their fingertips.

There are plenty of people in the world today who will tell you that you cannot "get through the door." Everywhere you turn you'll see signs that read "Do Not Enter." Somebody will always be happy to inform you, "Yes, God can save you from your sins, but the days of miracles are over. They're finished. The last round has been fought, and God's supernatural power fizzled out with the last of the apostles." For God to deliver all of us from that type of teaching is my prayer. The Jesus I know has miracles for us today.

The four men who took their friend to Jesus were rebuffed. All the doors were closed to them, but they refused to take no for an answer. Why? They believed they were coming to the end of an uphill climb.

What did they do? They hauled their friend, stretcher and all, onto the roof, and then they did something that was totally unorthodox. They began to tear the tiling off that roof one by one and then lowered the paralytic down into the crowd right in front of Jesus. In those days the roofs were made out of tiling, and it was easy to strip the tiles away. The four men literally began to raise the roof for victory. (Luke 5:19.)

Taking What's Rightfully Yours

I want you to imagine this scene from the Bible. The room is jammed to the rafters. Jesus Christ is preaching down heaven. All of a sudden the crowd gasps. Their attention is drawn toward the ceiling as a loud scratching noise comes from the roof. In the next split second, a trickle of dust begins to sift down onto their hair and faces. All at once a sparkle of sunlight flashes through the hole in the roof. Then the hole starts to widen, and Jesus glances up as the men begin to lower their friend down into the room on some kind of a cot or pallet.

I want you to notice what the Bible says next: "He [Jesus] saw *their* faith." Whose faith did He see? The faith of the man's four friends. When He sees the men's faith, He fastens His eyes on the paralyzed man and declares, "Your sins are forgiven." (v. 20.) Don't you think that was an unusual thing for the Lord to say? Here is a man who is paralyzed, his whole body limp and lifeless. He cannot take one single step alone, and yet Jesus proclaims, "Man, your sins are forgiven."

The Lord cut right through to the heart of the matter because He recognized that the man wasn't right with God. The man knew he wasn't right with God. When you and I get into the awesome, holy presence of Jesus, we can feel the Holy Spirit's microscope going over us. We know whether or not we need to get something straightened out with Him.

Jesus recognized that the man was "lost and undone, without God or His Son," as the gospel song "When He reached down His hand for Me" says. He told him, "Your sins are forgiven." In a lightning-like flash, the man's heart was transformed. His sins were washed away. His whole life was made brand new.

That episode caused quite an uproar among the religious leaders. After all, who does Jesus think He is to forgive a man's sins. Only God can forgive sins, they reasoned. The Bible says that the Lord perceived their thoughts. He asked them, "Which is easier, to say, 'Your sins be forgiven you,' or to say 'Rise up and walk'? But that you may know that the Son of God has power to forgive sins,' He said to the man who was paralyzed, 'I say to you, arise, take up your bed, and go to your house'" (Luke 5:22-24).

All of a sudden there was a special moment. There is always a special moment in your life and mine—a moment when we must put our faith in gear and act on the words of Jesus. The paralyzed man came to that special moment. He had to make a choice to act.

His friends had struggled to carry him to the top of an uphill climb. They knocked down every obstacle and raised the roof for victory. They lowered the man into the very presence of Jesus. The Lord had forgiven his sins, and then He cut through all the fat when He exclaimed, "Now take up your bed and walk." It was a special moment. It was up to the man to act.

The air was still. You could scarcely hear the sound of anyone breathing. Dust was still sifting down from the ceiling and dancing in the sunlight. Everyone shifted to the edge of their seats. They had heard the stories about the Man from Galilee. They had heard the rumors about this healing miracle-worker. They knew about the Lord, but now they're standing in His presence. The holy God of the universe was right before them, and the paralyzed man was there too. Jesus had delivered the Word. Now it was the man's turn to act.

There always comes a time when it's *your* turn to act. What are you going to do when Jesus lays the Word on you? Are you going to obey Him? Or are you going to mumble, "Well, now, let me think about it for a moment"? You've got to grab hold of your miracle the way a drowning man grabs for his last breath of air.

When Jesus gave the word to the paralyzed man, "Arise, take up your bed, and walk," everybody was gawking at him. Everybody was craning their necks, straining to see what would happen next. I can picture the reporters from the *Jerusalem Times* huddled over in one corner of the room with their little notepads. They were ready to roll the presses. They were positive they could make the syndicated news network if they only hurried. "Paralytic healed. Film at 11."

Now the ball is in the paralyzed man's court. Perhaps he muttered to himself, *Why shouldn't I go ahead and get up? I know I've been down for a long time, but I'm sick and tired of lying here on this bed of affliction. I want to get up and go home. I want to give my wife a great big hug. I want to run and play ball with my children for the first time in years.* In a moment's time, he decided to act on God's Word. All at once the miracle power of Jesus struck him like a bolt of lightning.

When the power of the Lord hits you and you respond to His power, a miracle can be transferred into your life.

In the flash of a second, his lifeless limbs surged with strength. He leaped to his feet, folded up his bed, and began to dance all around the room in a Holy Ghost Jericho March. Pandemonium broke loose in that house that day. There was an explosion of joy and a great celebration. The paralyzed man made it to the end of an uphill climb.

The End of Your Hill

It's important for you to reach out with your spirit and grab hold of the fact that you're coming to the end of an uphill climb. Aren't you glad that you're not caught on a downhill slide? God never takes you on a downhill slide. He always takes you on an uphill climb. You must act on God's Word like the paralyzed man did when his four friends took him to Jesus.

Remember what happened when the three young Hebrews, Shadrach, Meshach, and Abednego, were cast into Nebuchadnezzar's burning, fiery furnace? They didn't lie down and wallow in the flames. They didn't run around in circles and scream and shout. They started marching in the fire.

Why should you settle for living in hell the rest of your life? Don't you dare take a ticket. Don't you dare park in the valley. If your hope seems gone, don't give up. Keep your eyes on the Lord and realize that you're close to your victory.

Prayer of Salvation

God loves you—no matter who you are, no matter what your past is. God loves you so much that He gave His one and only begotten Son, Jesus, for you. The Bible tells us that "...whoever believes in him shall not perish but have eternal life" (John 3:16 NIV). Jesus laid down His life and rose again so that we could spend eternity with Him in heaven and experience His absolute best on earth. If you would like to receive Jesus into your life, pray the following prayer out loud and mean it from your heart.

Heavenly Father, I come to You admitting that I am a sinner. Right now, I choose to turn away from sin. I repent, and I ask You to cleanse me of all unrighteousness. I believe that Your Son, Jesus, died on the cross to take away my sins. I also believe that He rose again from the dead so that I might be forgiven of my sins and made righteous through faith in Him. I call upon the name of Jesus Christ to be the Savior and Lord of my life. Jesus, I choose to follow You and ask that You fill me with the power of the Holy Spirit. I declare that right now I am a child of God. I am free from sin and full of the righteousness of God. I am saved in Jesus' name. Amen.

If you prayed this prayer to receive Jesus Christ as your Savior for the first time, please contact us on the Web at **www.harrisonhouse.com** to receive a free book.

Or you may write to us at

Harrison House
P.O. Box 35035
Tulsa, Oklahoma 74153

About the Author

Richard Roberts, B.A., M.A., D.Min, has dedicated his life to minister the saving, healing, delivering power of Jesus Christ around the world. Since 1993 he has served as President of Oral Roberts University in Tulsa, Oklahoma. He is the CEO of Oral Roberts Evangelistic Association, co-chairman of International Charismatic Bible Ministries, and a member of ORU's Board of Regents.

Under his leadership as President, ORU has added new academic programs, reached the highest enrollment in its history, and received numerous gifts and grants. Richard Roberts is fully committed to ensuring that the future of ORU remains strong while keeping the God-ordained university true to its founding purposes of joining academics with the power of prayer, and healthy aerobics and physical fitness. He has been honored by being listed in *Who's Who Among University Presidents* and was voted an Alumnus of the Year for 1999 by the ORU Alumni Board.

Richard and his wife, Lindsay, host a nationally syndicated TV program, "The Hour of Healing"—a one-hour, interactive nightly broadcast that reaches out to millions. On this unique healing program, Richard and Lindsay minister in the power of the Holy Spirit, praying for those who are sick or hurting in some area of their lives, and often giving specific words of knowledge about how God is touching people with His healing power. "The Hour of Healing" has received tens of thousands of phone calls from viewers who have reported healing miracles.

Richard is a man on fire for God, consumed by the compassion of Jesus for sick and hurting people. He conducts healing rallies and crusades across the United States and around the world. Since his healing ministry began in 1980, he has ministered the healing power of Jesus on six continents. His meetings are marked by a tremendous move of the Spirit, resulting in all types and physical, mental, emotional, financial, and spiritual healings. "Jesus was born into a world of trouble to bring healing and deliverance," Richard states. "That is the call of God upon my own life—to reach out to people in their troubles and heartaches, to pray and believe God, and to bring His Word of hope and healing."

In addition to his responsibilities at ORU and OREA, Richard has authored a number of books, including his autobiography, *He's the God of a Second Chance,* which has been requested by more than half a million people.

A native Tulsan, Richard is very active in the local community. He has a strong commitment to the city of Tulsa and his vision for the university as part of the community.

Richard and Lindsay have three daughters—Jordan, Olivia, and Chloe.

For prayer requests or to contact Richard, write to:
Richard Roberts
7777 South Lewis Avenue
Tulsa, OK 74171

Prayer requests can also be emailed to:
prayer@orm.cc

For more information on ORU or the Oral Roberts Ministries,
log on to www.oru.edu or www.orm.cc

For prayer any time,
call the Abundant Life Prayer Group at 918-495-7777

www.harrisonhouse.com

Fast. Easy. Convenient!

◆ New Book Information
◆ Look Inside the Book
◆ Press Releases
◆ Bestsellers
◆ Free E-News
◆ Author Biographies

◆ Upcoming Books
◆ Share Your Testimony
◆ Online Product Availability
◆ Product Specials
◆ Order Online

For the latest in book news and author information, please visit us on the Web at www.harrisonhouse.com. Get up-to-date pictures and details on all our powerful and life-changing products. Sign up for our e-mail newsletter, *Friends of the House,* and receive free monthly information on our authors and products including testimonials, author announcements, and more!

Harrison House—
Books That Bring Hope, Books That Bring Change

The Harrison House Vision

Proclaiming the truth and the power
Of the Gospel of Jesus Christ
With excellence;

Challenging Christians to
Live victoriously,
Grow spiritually,
Know God intimately.